Scores of women must take credit for the authorship of this book. The small editorial committee involved in its final production is merely representative of the many who deserve credit.

About the Authors

Mary Ferris is a hospital domestic working part-time in the Royal Victoria Hospital. She is a founder member of the Health and History Project and a member of NUPE's Women's Committee. She started the project as a shop steward and is now the Union's national representative on the National Women's Advisory Committee.

Anna McGonigle is a schools meals worker from Omagh. She is a founder member of the Health and History Project and a long standing member of the Women's Committee in Northern Ireland. She started the project as a local branch secretary and is now Vice President of NUPE.

Patricia McKeown is a full-time organiser for NUPE and Secretary of the Women's Committee.

Theresa Moriarty is an Historian and member of the Irish Labour History Society in Dublin. She has worked with NUPE's Women's Committee since the inception of the project.

Marie Mulholland is a Community Worker in North and West Belfast. She is a NUPE Shop Steward and a long standing member of the Women's Committee.

4

Contents

Introduction

As women came together to get this short oral history ready for publication, the largest hospital in Northern Ireland cut all gynaecological operations by half. Women's health and well being is clearly still an expendable item.

This book is about the collective memories of women who have never been consulted in the decision-making processes which shape our world. Not consulted about their needs and desires, they have been accorded few rights. Here is the story of the invisible. It is the story of women who have struggled in the shadows so that *we* may come into the light. This is our attempt to bring them into the light with us.

As women, we know, but often take for granted, our capacity for struggle. We take it for granted because endurance as a way of life is a concept which has been handed down to us by generations of women. Men take it for granted because they put no value on our struggles. They rarely recognise them in the present and have always written them out of history. This short book is our small attempt to recover and reclaim our history.

The women we remember in this book have never had power but have always had responsibility. They had responsibility for their families and their communities and indeed for themselves. But for them responsibility for self always came last.

We pay homage to them. In rediscovering their history, our own lives have been profoundly touched. The very exercise of coming together as women in this project has given all of us a new sense of worth. By taking the opportunity to recall and value the lives of our mothers and grandmothers, we have also learned much about ourselves.

The book is written by women who have   their own battles. They are determined that they will not   en out of history. At the time of writing, many of them ha   their jobs through privatisation. Others have left work   are for their young children and cannot come back because of lack of childcare facilities. Many of them are still with us but the daily struggles increase.

We remember them all just as we remember the mothers, the grannies, the aunties and the handywomen who people this book.

We remember the joy and laughter of recalling our past, the righteous anger as women recognised the wrongs done to our families and the determination to fight against all the processes that try to make us invisible too. For our women there is a collective commitment to ensure that their daughters have a better future.

Inez McCormack
Divisional Officer

How we did it

Back in the early 1980s our Health and History project was born. It emerged out of a number of considerations and events which converged through NUPE's Women's Committee. It was a time, not unlike today, when cutbacks in the public service, particularly in health and education, were having a profound effect on the lives of ordinary women. NUPE women were at the receiving end, both as public service workers and as users of the service. Our jobs, our working conditions and our pay were being seriously affected. The quality of our lives and that of our families was being diminished as everything from school uniform grants and provision of free school meals, to increased prescription charges, diminishing access to hospital care and diminishing access to community care impacted upon us as a result of government policies.

Somewhere on the horizon loomed the threat of privatisation, but what it really meant and how it might really affect us all was not something that the NUPE members in Northern Ireland were immediately preoccupied with. We were too busily engaged in the daily struggle for survival.

Coincidentally, around this time some members of the Women's Committee travelled, with the Irish Labour History Society, to a conference of the Welsh Labour History Society, held in South Wales. The theme of the conference was the history of working class women. Those of us who took part thoroughly enjoyed the experience, but developed the idea that we should take responsibility for uncovering and making visible our own history as women. Instead of being the subject of historical study we were enthused by the idea of researching it for ourselves and we brought back these ideas to the union's Women's Committee.

One of the main responsibilities of the Women's Committee was to motivate women members to become involved in the life of our union. Many experiments in this direction had been tried since the late '70s and one which was proving most successful was the involvement of NUPE women in a series of one day seminars and weekend schools on the subject of women's health, which up till then had not been regarded by the outside world as a 'real' trade union issue.

'Dig where you stand'

The union's local education programme was developing and much of the inspiration for this programme came directly from the Women's Committee. For us it was a positive advantage that the officer who looked after the Women's Committee was also our Education officer.

She had recently returned from an Education Methods course at the Trades Union Congress in London, where a 'Dig where you stand' exercise had caught her imagination. The method used in 'Dig where you stand' is simple and exciting. A large flip chart is divided into sections, marked off as decades, and is then used to investigate the historical development of a chosen topic, from the knowledge and memory of any small group of people who choose to discuss it. Topics are written across the top of the flip chart and a group of four or five people start recounting memories from each of the decades. Key words are jotted down for each decade, and the findings are summarised at the end.

The 'Dig where you stand' method grabbed our imaginations too and soon all the components of what became the Health and History project came together in an exciting discussion at the Women's Committee.

We wanted to involve women members in the union. We wanted to find a way of motivating them to fight back against public service cutbacks and the threat of privatisation. We wanted to investigate and reclaim our own history. We knew that women's health was an issue near and dear to all our hearts, and now we had found a simple and exciting method of turning us into mistresses of our own history.

Our first step was to organise a workshop to explore our topic and to think about how we might involve other generations of women in our families - mothers, grandmothers and great-grandmothers. We chose a series of headings under the main title of women's health and history, which we felt would focus our project. These were:

Family Health
Housing and diets
Official and unofficial health care
Childbirth and contraception
Sex

First steps

Our first 'Dig where you stand' exercise was inspirational. The room was full of women who ranged from post-National Health Service babies who had never really thought about the struggle of their own families to create a health service, through to women who had vivid memories of the days before the NHS when life or death was a hit and miss affair, and survival depended on the goodwill and special knowledge of the local handywoman and the support of family and friends.

The exercise created in us a feeling of urgency. As the knowledge unfolded of the struggles of our mothers and grandmothers, we realised how much more there was to discover about our own history as women; and how little time there was left to uncover it as the generation which was keeper of the knowledge fast disappeared.

In the same workshop we explored methods for recapturing and recording this knowledge, before it was lost forever. We devised a series of questions to ask our mothers, grandmothers and other women in our families and experimented there and then with such questions, and possible answers, against a background of much laughter and tears.

A third element of this first workshop was to think about how we might gain access to other primary source material for our project. Women identified libraries, old newspapers records and mothers' attics as likely sources. Others thought about people in the local community who might be able to help: retired midwives

13

and district nurses, school teachers and local handywomen.

Our aim was to gather the information for ourselves and to involve as many as possible of our women members and their families in the collective exercise of rediscovering our past. We did not at this stage have the ambitious idea of producing a book of oral history. That came much later.

Development of leadership

In a series of similar workshops over the next couple of years the number of women taking part grew rapidly. Our confidence developed and deepened.

Each time we held a workshop we saw it as an end in itself and we still do. Women who participated in the 'Dig where you stand' exercise were enriched and invigorated as they recalled the struggles of their mothers and grandmothers and, more often than not, their own struggles. The stark contrasts between life before and after the foundation of the welfare state became more and more obvious and there was the constant identification of life turning full circle - not for the better, but for the worse - as we became more acutely aware of the destruction of the same services which had made women's lives more bearable.

Several campaign issues emerged from the workshops. Particular problems such as the termination of free school meals, the burden of growing prescription charges, and cutbacks in the local hospital were seen as campaign issues. Many members of the Women's Committee went on to play leading roles in these campaigns, motivating NUPE members with their enthusiasm and their insight.

Other women chose to campaign on current women's health issues and to start making demands of their GPs, their local hospital and their employers.

The issue of privatisation ceased to be a theoretical concept which the union's activists were expected to discuss every so often. Instead it came to be seen as a real threat, particularly to women, at work and in the community. In later years many of the women who took their first faltering steps in the union through the Health and History project became leaders of the

14

campaigns against cuts and privatisation. We had succeeded in one of our major aims, that of involving women and developing their confidence to become activists.

Travelling out

Word soon got out that something exciting was happening inside NUPE and other women wanted to see for themselves how the project worked.

At an early stage the Irish Labour History Society invited us to run a workshop on Women's Health and History at an Irish Labour History conference in Trinity College, Dublin. We were thrilled at the invitation and extremely nervous at the prospect. This time we would not only be the subject of the discussion; we would also be historians revealing our primary source discoveries.

Some of us 'volunteered' to deliver the 'lecture' and many examples of oral history discovered through our flip chart method were displayed at the conference. We realised then that we needed to be more rigorous in recording the material that was pouring out of our regular workshops.

In later workshops we enlisted the aid of new technology. We videoed report-backs and we used tape recorders to capture not only the report-backs, but the flip chart discussions in the small groups themselves.

When we decided that we wanted to publish an oral history pamphlet we refined the workshops and held a number of intensive weekends. We concentrated on more specific subjects where we felt information was sparse. All of this activity was recorded to enable us to build up a bank of oral history from which the material in this book has been drawn.

We have taken our experimental workshops to conferences in London and Dublin and we have enlarged them in Northern Ireland to include women from the community.

Many years ago we invited women from SIPTU to join us in a Health and History workshop in Derry. It created a bond between women from all parts of Ireland, a bond which grows stronger with the passing years.

We have run several of the workshops with women from the community in Belfast and in Derry. We have always had close links with them but the Health and History exercise made us sisters and friends.

When in 1988 we took our workshop to London to the Women Alive conference, we found women of all creeds, race and political backgrounds submerging their differences and celebrating their history. It made us proud.

Each time we have used the same format and it has never failed to prove that within every one of us the history of our mothers' struggles is imprinted. It simply takes the focus of the 'Dig where you stand' exercise to bring out much of our history. We do it all the time. You can do it too.

Mary Ferris
Anna McGonigle
Patricia McKeown
Theresa Moriarty
Marie Mulholland

Childbirth and childhood

Falls Road Belfast Hospital for Sick Children, 1933

The tracing of the history of women's health in Northern Ireland, learnt from the stories of women relatives, took the project back to the start of the century. We traced the three generation span of living memory, from the birth and childhood of our grandmothers, and gradually built up, decade by decade, a graphic history of women's lives. Each part of the process would record a personal event from among the families that the women represented.

Thus emerged a general picture of women's lives, punctuated by individual stories that confirmed, or perhaps contradicted, the general picture.

Home births in the early 1900s

Kathleen, a home help whose grandmother, mother and herself were all born in the same house in Belfast, gave the following account of changes in childbirth treatments, practices and customs through the years. It is a startling summary from her own and other women's memories and experiences, recounted in their groups.

In the 1900s to the 1920s most children were born at home, and there was a handywoman in every area. There was no such thing as a midwife. There was always somebody there, a couple of streets away. She would be called on to help with your mammy having a baby.

A lot of girls who weren't married had babies. This used to happen frequently on the farms. The old lad would have his way with them, and they got the sack once they got pregnant. That was mentioned by the women from Omagh, as well as from Belfast, in the group discussion. It's what both sides did, you know.

There were no prams or cots in those days. There was an orange or tomato box for the child, and the children were put into the corner most of the time. To get about, the child was wrapped in the shawl. There were baby binders to support the baby's back, which are not used now. Sometimes they put a penny on the baby's belly button and thrust round this big binder.

There was post-natal depression, but there wasn't a name for it. Women were put away in the asylum. It was taken that they were gone around the twist. Sometimes, women were put away if they were having a baby and weren't married. That was a disgrace. You were put away for that sort of thing.

An awful lot of mothers and babies died. Maybe they were having some difficulty that could now be prevented. Then it ended up that the mother and child both died.

Women were very ignorant about having babies. They just went along with it. They were having a baby, and they didn't really know what was happening from the start to the finish of it.

Some people thought, really thought, that a good way of stopping having another baby, was to feed the baby themselves. They couldn't get pregnant if they were breast feeding the baby.

Babies then didn't really walk as early as they do now. A baby nowadays is on its feet at nine months. It was believed then that if a child walked too soon, it would get bandy legged. They thought its wee legs would crumple down underneath it.

In the 1930s they introduced the district nurse. The district nurse had to be paid for, and the doctor as well. There was no such thing as a mother staying in bed for long, say five days or so, after having the baby. She had a baby and hours after that she was up making the dinner for the husband coming home from work.

In the country babies were sometimes born in the fields, where the mother was out working. The baby was put in a wee box and the mother just went on working.

This was not a generalisation from the early part of the century. Kathleen emphasised that her account was drawn from the first fifty years of their memories.

We're not really talking about the early part of the century. It appears right down to the 1950s. All this sort of thing was happening until the health service began.

High mortality rates

Family memories of childbirth in the north of Ireland from the beginning of this century confirmed and expanded this grim picture. Childbirth and infancy were so dangerous that a baby survived almost, it seems, against the odds. The danger of both mother and baby dying was high, as many stories confirmed.

The death toll of women in childbirth at the start of the century was relentless.

Three grandmothers of the women in our group died in childbirth. Iris was told her grandmother had died from puerperal fever (a form of blood poisoning caused by infection during childbirth) which was then quite common. None of our mothers or our immediate relatives died in childbirth.

Marie, a community worker in Belfast, whose grandmother and mother all come from the same district in the north of the city, had a great aunt, Jenny, her granny's sister, who died in childbirth. Margaret, a Craigavon nurse, had a grandmother who died in childbirth.

And back to work

Anne, a part-time cleaner from Coleraine, and the granddaughter of a Co Derry agricultural worker, gave examples from her family of the 1920s and 1930s.

My granny's sister's wains were born in the workhouse. An aunt of my mummy's gave birth in a field, and went back to work right away. See, in the country areas you had to go back to work the next day. My (great) aunt was back at work the same day.

Anna, a school meals worker from Omagh, gave a similar account from her district, in the 1930s.

Lily's mother went back to work in the fields three days later, with Lily beside her in a sort of play-pen, a tea chest.

But it was not just countrywomen who had such short confinements, or none at all. Few families could afford a wage earner to be off work for long. Industrial women workers experienced the same urgency.

Mary, a Belfast hospital domestic, whose grandmother and mother were mill workers, recalled the city pattern.

The women in Belfast worked immediately after childbirth. Most of them just had their babies and went back to work within days. They couldn't afford to take time off.

Not only family memories record this practice. Medical officers in the city report it as commonplace.

... mothers work in the mills and factories to within a few days of the birth of children, and return to work again as soon as their employers will permit (Belfast Medical Officer of Health, 1906).

At this time employers were obliged by law to see that their women workers took time off before childbirth, and that they did not return to work for four weeks after giving birth. This was customarily overlooked by mutual agreement between mothers and employers. Such short confinements were not due to medical opinion or practice, but because of the necessity of keeping a regular wage coming into the house, as their granddaughters' reports make clear.

Maternity services in the north of Ireland were meagre or non-existent at the turn of the century. Only Belfast in the north of Ireland had a maternity hospital, which dated from the 1800s. Midwives were scarce. In 1901 only three are recorded in the Derry city census and none in the county. Such midwives were employed by the workhouse infirmary.

Though family memories of childbirth deaths are high, the overall statistics for Ireland were considered to be low. Health officials at the time believed this was because Irish figures were notoriously inaccurate, since there was no effective law to register births and deaths at the time. Babies' deaths in childbirth were simply not recorded in either the birth or death register. Since it cost money to register both births and deaths, there was little incentive for a poor family to have such a tragedy recorded.

The handywoman

Kathleen's account of childbirth in her grandmother's generation introduced the figure of the handywoman. Other women's information testified to the handywoman's enduring assistance at births throughout the years. For most women, she was usually the only experienced help available during birth.

Our grandmothers' births range from 1876 to 1900, and all without exception were home births. There were no doctors present.

We can't recall any medicine used for women giving birth. There was a handywoman and water boiled on the range.

The handywoman was the main help that any woman had when she was giving birth. The handywoman was not just there in the 1900s. She was there right down to the 'sixties. In the 'fifties handywomen and the district nurse worked hand in hand.

Medical officials blamed handywomen delivering babies in the home for the deaths of mothers from infection. More realistic observers today suggest that handywomen were probably no more blameworthy than doctors, who came from other homes or hospital wards where they treated a wide range of infectious diseases, without the hygiene practices taken for granted today.

Childhood diseases

A baby girl, or her brother, faced the most dangerous year of her life in her first twelve months. If she survived birth itself, a range of infectious diseases threatened her health, and even her life. Seven of these were so widespread and dangerous that doctors had to report each case they saw to the local health officer. Smallpox and typhus were among the killer diseases at the start of this century.

But more common or persistent diseases left the greatest mark on family memories. Scarlet fever and whooping cough were also notifiable diseases. They were so frequent and deadly that both, along with measles, can be found among the less serious ailments for which there were home remedies or 'cures'.

Whooping cough: The child was put three times under a donkey or brought to the gasworks.
Ringworm: A widow rubbed her ring on the infected area.
Boils: A mixture of bread, water and washing soda was placed on the boil to draw out the infection. This was called a poultice. Another cure was to fill a bottle with warm water, and place the neck over the boil. This was supposed to draw out the infection.
Cholic: A hot cinder was taken out of the fire, and put in water; then strained off and the water was drunk.
Measles: Sulphur was added to a taste of whiskey, and the concoction was drunk.

24

At a time when hospitals did not, in normal circumstances, admit infants it is not surprising to find childhood diseases among those listed for home 'cures'. A walk to the gasworks with a baby suffering whooping cough would be a well-tried remedy where no alternative treatments were available.

Diphtheria is remembered as a deadly disease at the turn of the century. It was infectious, fatal, and afflicted the very young.

If she were born in Belfast, though, a baby was more likely to fall sick and die from diarrhoea. She was thought to be more at risk of dying from diarrhoea if her mother was working.

The mortality is almost always higher where female labour is largely employed, as is the case in Belfast. A large number of mothers find it necessary to go out to work and leave their children in charge of some old woman, who is usually paid a small consideration.

Under these circumstances it is not difficult to believe that infant life suffers to a considerable extent through ignorance of how food should be prepared, as well as allowing the child to remain in a state of filthy and unhealthy surroundings (Belfast Medical Officer of Health, 1906).

Move towards hospital births

We discovered that two baby clinics had been opened in Belfast as far back as 1908. One was in Divis Street and the other in Ballymacarett. Neither was run by the council. Both were maintained, with a nurse and a doctor, by women's health campaigners, the Women's National Health Association.

It took the first world war, the deaths of thousands of soldiers and a falling British birth rate for the authorities to become alarmed at the state of women's health and infant welfare.

The Carnegie Trust, a charitable research body which was commissioned to investigate both, introduced its report with the stark findings that more babies died in their first twelve months than did soldiers at the front. The report, published in 1917, showed that Irish infant deaths were declining slower than elsewhere, that the death rates for children at school were worse than for infants, and that one third of the women who died after childbirth had been stricken with puerperal fever.

The report proposed that councils' health authorities be given more powers to set up health services for women and children. Such centralised efforts made little impact, as councillors were not obliged to supply the services, and these powers remained largely unused. The only measure that was enforced was the medical inspection of children in national schools.

The report proposed there should be more hospital births. Our family memories revealed that very few of our grandmothers were born in hospital. But where there were special health circumstances there were some hospital births.

Anne, from County Derry, told how her grandmother had given birth in a hospital in 1933.

> *She had mammy when she was fifteen. She didn't marry the father, because he would not admit to being the father. It was 1933 when my mammy was born, so they took my granny into hospital in case there were any complications. At the time they were usually born at home. It was the Mary Rankin, a maternity hospital. It's knocked down now.*

Women whose own lives or whose babies' lives were thought to be at risk, were brought into hospital to give birth. Marie remembered,

> *My mother was born in 1938, and she was definitely born in hospital, because my nanny had already lost four children, and she knew all the births were really difficult. So she was brought to hospital for my mother's birth.*

The hungry 'thirties

Hospital births were still exceptions in the 1930s. But even for healthy mothers, or women whose births seemed to threaten no complications, childbirth was a traumatic and exhausting experience.

Margaret, a Craigavon nurse, described the treatment of women during childbirth before widespread maternal care was introduced.

My mother told me you wouldn't get any dinner before childbirth. For about two or three days you got tea and toast. They treated you like an invalid. Do you know in those days, there were big iron railings with brass knobs on the bed. Well, the handywoman tied a towel on the railings and this is what my mother pulled on.

My mother says there was one birth she thought she wouldn't get through and it was 7/6d to bring the doctor. She said all she could think of was that 7/6d - what it would buy for us in food for the next week. And she kept saying to the nurse, 'Don't get him yet. It might be all right. Don't get him yet', because she was didn't want to spend the 7/6d. She was actually risking her life.

In the 1930s, birth still held its dangers or led to severe health conditions.

We had another aunt who died after giving birth. The womb closed over the afterbirth and it scattered through her. She died very shortly afterwards.

Women who had given birth could get 'milk leg', a condition which arose, some thought, if the mother was not feeding a baby herself, and was laid up for too long.

The milk used to go through people and kill them. But they've developed pills. I don't know if anyone here ever got them: wee red, pinky ones, which did away with this milk leg.

During the 1930s, life for women worsened. The death rates in childbirth were falling in Britain and also in Ireland. In

27

Northern Ireland they increased. By 1938 a woman was more likely to die in childbirth than in 1923. By 1940 more babies died in childbirth than had ever been previously recorded. The hungry 'thirties in Northern Ireland took a huge toll on the lives of young mothers and children. In this way we can see how women bore the brunt of the depression years.

National Health Service

When in 1948 the National Health Service was introduced into Northern Ireland, all women were for the first time brought into the health care system. The greatest impact of this change was on mothers, with its new emphasis on maternity care and welfare.
   Kathleen records developments under the welfare state.

The health service started to come in, in the 1950s, with maternity grants. The thalidomide drug for morning sickness caused a lot of deformities in babies.

Ante-natal and post-natal clinics were set up and the use of contraceptives resulted in smaller families. It was all more or less big families before. People got wiser then. In the 1960s to 1970s they brought out the pill, so they did, and sex education was taught in the schools.

A mother had to stay a certain time in hospital, maybe six days or so. And six weeks after the baby was born, you went back for your post-natal.

You got tablets, if you weren't feeding your baby, to scatter the milk. Breast feeding has started to come back again. They're even having places in hotels and airports for the women to go, whereas before, the women would've gone and hidden away. They would be embarrassed at the idea of feeding the baby.

Now in the 1980s, we're going back to the 1930s, when the health service is running down again. They prefer women to have their babies at home, to save money.

Things changed with the welfare state, and a whole range of benefits came in: the maternity grant (although this hasn't changed since the day and the hour it was introduced), free milk, orange juice and malt.

Some of us recalled a rise in hospital births in our families, with the introduction of the NHS, although this experience was not uniform. Mary was born in the City hospital in Belfast, because her mother's first child had died.

It has been almost all hospital births since the NHS in the 1940s. But in Kathleen's family (Belfast) fourteen were born at home and only one in hospital. The last one in Rosaleen's family (Belfast) was born in hospital in 1952. In Anne's (Derry) all six were born at home between 1948 and 1959. Eileen's first was born in a nursing home in 1953. The second was born in hospital a year later, and the other four were born at home.

The rise in hospital births, viewed by the medical profession as making childbirth safer, was not universally welcomed by women. Kathleen's mother retained strong reservations.

As far as my mother heard, it was rough, and they didn't treat you right. At the beginning when women had babies in hospital, they were treated like animals.

Infants were protected against the deadly childhood infections by an increasing variety of inoculations, which started with smallpox, diphtheria, scarlet fever and whooping cough jabs and came to include polio, measles, and for young women, rubella or German measles.

Developments in the 'sixties

It was twenty years before a more comprehensive health system was introduced in the schools. Free books and materials, school meals and milk, medical and dental inspection and treatment, special provision for handicapped children, nursery schools, school transport, scholarships and further education - everything that had been so conspicuously neglected in the past was now provided.

At school there was a new emphasis on physical education.

In our time (the 1960s) it was netball and ball games. Most people remembered bean-bags at primary school. We really had only exercise yards.

In the primary school there were hoola-hoops and bean bags. Camogie was played in the park, in the summer. Rounders were played and we had to wear navy knickers. At secondary school PE was far better as there were better facilities. Gym frocks were worn there.

School nurse inspections to monitor children's health had become a regular part of school life. Sarah, from Derry, recalled her memories of the school nurse's visit, and the lack of privacy that children experienced.

If there was anything wrong with your hair, your name was taken and you were shown up in front of everyone. Then a letter went to your parents and you had to use a solution to clean the hair.

Other women recalled similar experiences from school days, when soap was issued to children whose hair was not clean. Margaret remembers:

One girl was given the soap to wash her hair, and because her hair was not clean, her mother received a summons to go to court.
The checks for headlice were done in the classroom, and the nurse also checked for ringworm and impetigo. If you had any of these you got a letter to go to the clinic for treatment. Rosaleen remembers having impetigo, and she thought it was great getting time off school.

The nurse checked for headlice in front of the whole

30

class, using two knitting needles and a bowl of disinfectant. Anyone who didn't pass would get a ticket to go to the clinic for treatment. One girl had to have her head shaved and she wore a hat.

Childbirth and childcare today

The entire experience of childbirth and infancy, constructed by these memories, has changed today. Babies are born in hospitals, not homes. Medical teams, including a doctor, have replaced the handywoman.

Although childbirth in our lifetimes moved into high technology, some of the conveyor belt attitude that came with it has now receded. One woman told how her daughter could 'sit, stand or squat'. 'Our Deborah had the choice to have it anyway she wanted'; although such flexibility by the hospitals was seen as rare.

Epidurals, the painkilling injections into a woman's spinal cord covering, which numbed her from the waist down, have been stopped. We recalled horror stories associated with injections that went wrong.

The more natural methods of childbirth, which rely on gas and air to assist breathing through labour pains, are used more commonly today, although some women in our groups remained suspicious of these.

They were also deeply suspicious about the medical motives for inducing births. Some women believe that decisions to induce were based more on the hospital's or doctor's convenience, than on the mother's relief. There had been a high rate of inductions during the 1970s.

Fathers have traditionally been absent at births, and few women expressed any enthusiasm for the practice of having them there, believing it was the hospitals, rather than women themselves, who encouraged it. 'Most women cried out for their mothers', their questioning revealed.

Some of the practices of childbirth have come full circle. Today women who want a home birth will be listened to more sympathetically, even though it would be generally discouraged.

The greatest of all changes today, as these family memories recount so clearly, is that in contrast to our grandmothers' days, women and babies survive childbirth, and a child, safely born, can be expected to grow up to adulthood, with an expectation of a full life span ahead of her.

Health care

Union Infirmary (now City Hospital), Lisburn Road, pre-1909.

At the start of this century, medical care was almost non-existent for the bulk of the population in Northern Ireland. Death was overwhelming due to infectious diseases. There were no antibiotics. Deadly infections could be nursed but not treated. Surgery was still not developed enough to deal with most of the conditions it treats today. Hygiene was acknowledged, but little practised in routine medical care. Hospitals, where they existed, provided the minimum of medical care for illnesses that were mainly untreatable.

Before the National Health Service was introduced, medical services for those who could not afford to buy them were provided through the poor law, administered by the local government board and the local authorities. Such services were funded by the ratepayers.

The two main institutions of the poor law were the workhouse, with its infirmary, and the dispensary service which employed a network of salaried doctors who dispensed medicines and made house calls within a district, at a set fee, or in some instances free of charge.

Precise details of medical services at the beginning of the century were not, it seems, part of family memories. But the memory of the workhouses survived their transformation into regional hospitals, and the incorporation of the buildings into the National Health Service.

The workhouse and the dispensary

Kathleen's memories of the workhouse were as follows:

The workhouse was more or less whispered about by my mother and my grandmother. They wouldn't have told you openly what it was. But later on we found out that it was for fallen women and destitute people. It was used as a

35

sort of hospital, because in those days there wasn't really a genuine hospital. The one that I remember is actually now Lurgan hospital. They were old stone buildings and very dark, dingy places. You wouldn't have got a private ward. They were all dormitories and old iron beds and things like that.

She recalls the dispensary service:

I came from a rural area, and the dispensary was in the doctor's surgery. I mean, after the doctor had seen you he went through this wee curtain where he had all these shelves of bottles and he made you up this mixture. I must say that most times I went to the doctor it was always a dark red bottle he gave me. It didn't matter what complaint I had. He'd give me this dark red bottle. I don't know what was in it. It was rotten too. If you were sick, you went to the doctor and got a bottle. Farmers paid with chicken, eggs and jam. We had to survive without the doctor a lot of the time.

Mary, a hospital canteen worker from Belfast, gave another stark picture of the workhouse and the sense of stigma that set workhouse inmates apart from the rest of society.

The workhouse was sometimes known as the poorhouse. It was for the homeless and for women who fell by the wayside. Hair was cropped very close and rough material was used for the suits worn by the boys. Underwear was not worn. Suits didn't have any pockets. You weren't allowed to use toilets after workhouse people had used them, because these people were purged every morning. They were generally treated badly. Women who were pregnant had to work until the babies were born. Usually, people who went to the workhouse never left it until they died. Children of inmates were made to work very hard in the laundries and were brought up in the workhouses.

36

Dora remembered about the dispensary, that you got a white piece of paper and you went to this place and they just gave you medicine. They seemed to give you medicine for everything.

Rosaleen's group recalls the same social isolation that the workhouse inspired.

We did not know a lot about the workhouse. We were going on what we remembered being told years ago. The grandmothers would've known more about that.

Most of them were placed on the outskirts of the city, so when any working class people had to go into a workhouse, you very seldom got anyone going in to visit them. The buildings were never sited in working class areas. They were always sited outside the cities.

But most of the workhouses became local general hospitals. The one on the Lisburn Road is now the City hospital. The one in Derry is a general hospital now too. We discovered that some of the workhouses had isolation huts, which were sectioned off for the treatment of different infectious diseases. People were terrified of having to go to the workhouse. There was a stigma attached to it. People who spent time in a workhouse were treated very badly afterwards. Others didn't want to know about them at all.

We discovered that dispensaries were simply the offices where doctors made up their own medicines. We had a great discussion on whether or not the dispensaries were actually free. Some of them obviously were, in our grandmothers' days. But we can remember the one on Divis Street. The doctor actually charged sixpence. He had a wee container full of disinfectant and the patient had to drop the sixpence into the disinfectant, before the doctor would handle the money. We just couldn't remember whether all the dispensaries were free or not.

The killer diseases

What health services did exist were built up around the treatment of infectious diseases. The local authorities developed a two-pronged approach to the problem of infectious diseases: isolation of the victims, and public health works such as improvements to urban water supplies and sewage schemes. These initiatives made little impact in a largely rural population, where water was drawn from wells, and where the disposal of sewage and other waste was left to the householder. Even in the larger urban centres, privies were the only method of disposal available to the poorer householders.

People hospitalised with infectious diseases were isolated in the separate wards of the workhouse infirmary huts. Families with a TB sufferer were expected to build separate airy cabins or balcony extensions for the infected relative, and to leave windows open at night.

One of the few direct interventions by the authorities in the 1900s was in response to the 1902 smallpox outbreak in Belfast. Purdeysburn was opened as a fever hospital, and was regarded at the time as the most modern infectious diseases hospital in the kingdom. Typhoid deaths were so great in Belfast, that no other city or town in the United Kingdom equals or even approaches it.

Birth and death happened in the home. Sickness, no matter how severe, was nursed in the home. While a family would be powerless to prevent disease, injury, or epidemic entering the home, family members had to assume full responsibility for nursing.

Costs, cures and works of charity

Not only did women bear this total nursing responsibility, but their own vulnerability to ill-health was largely untouched by medical care.

Medical care was unavailable to the working class because they could not afford it. People just helped one another. But if someone was seriously ill, especially a child, they would call the doctor. They would also call the doctor if the bread-winner was ill. They would try and get the money to have that person seen to, to ensure a quick return to work.

Women who survived the history of ill-health recalled the hardship illness brought to families unable to meet the cost of treatment. They shared these memories with the women in the project.

Housecalls from the doctor cost 2/6d, and it was hard to raise the money, so he was rarely called. The doctor was called to the house only when there was serious illness. There was no hospitalisation then. (Interview by Ann, a worker in the blood transfusion service.)

A 79 year old woman had nursed her family at home during the 1918 Big 'Flu.

Nancy nursed her mother, brother and sister during the Big 'Flu and they all survived. She was lucky to avoid it herself. (The 1918 influenza epidemic killed millions of people world-wide. Interview by Mary, a Belfast hospital worker, with her neighbour.)

The need to take responsibility for caring for serious illness, without proper means or training, meant not only a common reliance on each other, but also a recourse to cures.

People depended on older remedies. Years ago, no matter what was wrong with you, you had a bottle for everything.

There was medical care for people who could afford it and charity for those who could not. You got a cough bottle for everything, from mumps to TB. It was sixpence, so the bigger the bottle, the better. The longer it lasted.

People used their own form of fumigation, sulphur candles. They still depended on the handywoman for childbirth and the washing of the dead, and old fashioned

39

remedies for serious illness.

If a family member died, neighbours stepped in to help with the crisis, even in preparations for burial.

Mary, a Belfast hospital canteen worker, remembers her grandmother.

At the age of fifteen my grandmother washed her first dead person. This was done free. It was known as one of the 'corporal works of mercy' (charity). So if anyone died they came for my grandmother to wash and have them ready for burial. She also visited the sick, and used to wash and get them ready for the priest coming. This could happen at any time of the day or night, and she was always ready to go. Also at the washes they used to play games and tricks and have music and songs.

The woman who washed the dead for her neighbours might often be the local handywoman as well.

The Women's National Health Association

Women recalled home cures for sickness and ill-health. But there was no popular memory of health campaigns by organisations like the Women's National Health Association (WNHA), founded in 1907. Research by Anna in the Omagh public library turned up a 1912 newspaper account of an Omagh branch meeting of the WNHA, addressed by the secretary of the Tuberculosis Committee.

The association made huge efforts in the field of maternal health and TB treatments. They were responsible for opening the first sanatoria in Ireland. But much of their work was eventually taken over by the local authorities, which probably accounts for why the WHNA activities have left no lasting trace in older family members' memories, in contrast to today's awareness of campaigning women's welfare groups.

Margaret, a Craigavon nurse, reported that her group did not remember any campaigning groups from the past.

Well, in the old days, we didn't know of any. Nowadays we have the well-woman clinics, rape crisis centres, the gingerbread groups, and the Mater Dei hostel for unmarried mothers, the Sally Ann (Salvation Army) places for unmarried mothers, places for battered wives and NUPE.

A similar list of today's women's organisations was given by Rosaleen, a Belfast hospital worker, reflecting on the limited services available to women in the past.

Now we have the well-woman clinics, women's aid and different women's organisations that are interested in women's health and are actually pushing for changes for women. Whereas in our grandmothers' and our mothers' day they wouldn't have had any of this type of help. The only thing they would've had were charity organisations. We had a good discussion in our group about this. In the better off classes the women didn't have very much to do, except sit on a committee and dispense charity to the poor. Unfortunately, they decided what you got and what you didn't get.

And she summed up two generations of health care.

There wasn't really a great deal of difference between the grandmothers and the mothers. We had the free dispensaries until the National Health Service took off, and we also had handywomen. In fact, I think there is still a handywoman about, even now. There's somebody you go to, someone who's been a nurse, or is still nursing.

Government from Stormont 1921

The profile of women's health and all the aspects of life that would have had a bearing on it showed little evidence of change with the shift to direct government from Stormont in 1921. Lives remained hard. There were no reforms or extensions of the health services even though Northern Ireland had been at the bottom of every health league table for decades. Some minor administrative changes took place. Union or workhouse infirmaries were converted to district hospitals in 1921. Northern Ireland in 1921 had the highest mortality rate in relation to England, Wales, Scotland and the Irish Free State.

No priority was given to health by the new Stormont governors. There was no Ministry of Health in the new line-up, despite the appalling record of the past. Health matters came under the local government ministry, where ratepayers' considerations were paramount.

Movement for change

But gradually, over time, the awareness of the need for a public health programme was developing in Northern Ireland. This was fuelled by the continuing and overwhelming threat from infectious diseases and by the self-interest of employers.

Margaret gave an account of this growing awareness, which led to the birth of the NHS, and told a personal story that illustrated how families and doctors faced the realities of chronic illness without the money to pay for treatment.

Well, we think that the administration gradually became interested because the working class people worked in the mills, and places like that, and it didn't suit employers to have them sick. They also worked in service in houses, and the high class people were looking for a better public health service to look after these people so that they would get on with their work. And there was a lot of infectious disease going about then, like TB, scarlet fever, meningitis, and things like that, and these people wouldn't have wanted you coming from a house where maybe these infections were.

In our discussions we went back to Aneurin Bevan. We know that he was a coal-miner, and watched miners die of silicosis, which was a lung disorder. When he was elected to parliament, to a labour government, he campaigned for a proper health service, free to all. And in the first year of the National Health Service thousands of pairs of glasses were given out. But you haven't heard it all! The glasses weren't so bad. Thousands of sets of false teeth were also given out!

When they first started the health service money wasn't very plentiful and they found out that they were going to have to put a bit of a charge on. So it was a shilling for a prescription, and 9/6d for glasses. It was 2/6d in my grandmother's day for the doctor to visit you. It was 7/6d in my mother's day. And then in my day, it was free. I didn't have to pay the doctor, thank goodness; I wouldn't have had the money.

I remember we had a family doctor, and you wouldn't get people like him around now. I had a brother who had a very bad chest, and every time the doctor would come to see him, my mummy would say, 'Make the bill up. Will you make the bill up?' And he would say, 'Yes. I'll make the bill up. I'll make the bill up.' And at the end, after about six visits, he would have made that bill up at 7/6d. That's the honest truth. It should have been actually pounds and pounds, you know. So that's just to let you know there was some humanity in those days. You don't get doctors like that anymore.

Rosaleen's group agreed with Margaret's points.

It was in their interests to have better public health, because any infectious diseases that were going about among the working class were carried to the upper class. Also, if people are ill they can't work properly. The working class has always been allowed enough comfort and medical care to keep them working. You know, you'll never get anymore than keeps you on the go.

Anna from Omagh also identified the decisive change of the

first post-war government.

The Labour Party came into power as a socialist government and they had promised medical care from the cradle to the grave.

The National Health Service

Women in our group discussions spelt out the first signs of the new health service at work, describing them as both innovative and enlightened.

District nurses visited the homes of the sick and bedridden. Visits to GPs and dentists were now free. Old age pensioners were given concessions. Free dinners were given to poor children. Children's health began to show an improvement.

Once there were changes we found women's disorders were brought out into the open and we realised that operations, especially mastectomies and hysterectomies, could save lives. At one time a hysterectomy was only for middle class or upper class women. The working class were not considered.

Cancer was brought out into the open too. Up till then it was 'Ah, she has cancer'. The word created fear, and that's why it was whispered about.

Nor were the changes limited to physical well-being. One woman recalled a decisive change for her family.

The handicapped and mentally ill were brought out of the dark, and it wasn't a disgrace to have someone in the house who wasn't the full shilling. That's just what it had been. A disgrace. Day centres were established, usually on a local basis, and specialist doctors were brought in.

44

The full medical

When we considered the availability to women of a comprehensive service to monitor women's health in the light of today's chronic rather than infectious illnesses, our discussions highlighted a gap in the health service. Few, if any, had ever had a 'medical' to monitor their health for employment or pregnancy. Most agreed it would have been almost entirely unknown in previous generations.

Mary, a Belfast canteen worker, recorded her group's discussion on the subject.

None of our grandmothers had a full medical, and if they fell into bad health they called on the handywoman who lived in the district. Mary's mother had a full medical. My mother had a full medical. But the rural people's mothers didn't have it. Women worked long hours and kept the home going, and that resulted in premature illness and death.

We all had a full medical, but there was a wee bit of a discussion in the group about what a full medical was. We didn't really know what could be classed as a full medical. What do you class as a full medical? Some thought a chest X-ray and a blood sample test was a full medical. But others of us wouldn't agree.

Rosaleen's group provided a similar picture.

I wouldn't say my grandmother ever had a full medical. My mother? No. I thought I had a medical, a full medical, but then as you say, if you have a chest X-ray and your blood pressure taken, that doesn't necessarily mean a medical. The only medical I have ever had I had to pay for, and I had to have it because my employer insisted on it. At that time everyone had to have it.

Rosaleen and Anna told of their experiences with full medicals.

We were told to go and pay for it, and that we would be reimbursed; of course we never were. We had a good discussion in our group about what exactly a full medical is. A full medical is not available on the NHS. You have to pay for it.

In the Education and Library Board, when I started twenty-two years ago, I was told it was compulsory to have a medical. I'm still waiting for mine. They obviously don't think health is important in the Educational and Library Boards.

The full medical was one subject that created an awful lot of discussion in our group. What is a full medical? When you go for a job you have to have it. Not for your own peace of mind, but for your employer's sake.

Into the future

Thinking about future services, Anna spoke for her group.

We would like to see women having a full free medical every year. When I say a full medical, I mean a full medical. Tests for cervical cancer and breast cancer should be included. We would like to see better pediatric and geriatric care, and more preventive medicine. We want better cradle to the grave facilities.

All the other women endorsed this view in their hopes for the future.

More funding for the health service is needed, more care for the elderly, more district nurses, more health visitors. We feel that a home help is a must to an old person living alone. But at the same time, too much should not be expected of a home help. They should not be left to take the place of a district nurse, or a health visitor.

Kathleen mentioned that she goes to visit an old man who is on a nebuliser (a breathing aid), and the nebuliser lasts about twenty minutes.

He has to have that three times a day. And yet there's never a health visitor or a district nurse to help out.

And we felt there should be more consideration for expectant mothers. Women are greatly embarrassed when they go to an ante-natal clinic, because you're sent in to one room to put on a gown, and then you're sent somewhere else. And you actually spend half a day there, and in some cases you spend longer than half a day.
We'd like to see more female doctors. A lot of hospitals are old and need updating. And we'd like to see better wages and conditions for the staff who work in the hospitals. We need better casualty facilities where people don't have to wait so long. You find that in most hospitals, no matter how big they are, there is only one casualty officer, and people have to wait for hours and hours.

Food and diet

Two girls planting seed potatoes, Glenshesk, Co. Antrim.

At the turn of the century, food was simple and basic. Town dwellers and country people shared a similar diet. Memories of the food our grandmothers ate or served up were recalled and compared with the food eaten by the family today.

Dora, a part-time cleaner in Coleraine, recalls,

In the old days it was mainly potatoes, porridge, home made soups and home baked bread. My grandmother had her own fresh vegetables growing in the garden. We had a half acre. And she also had an orchard at the corner, belonging to a farmer who gave it to her to use. We didn't lack for fresh fruit and vegetables. Well, my mother was similar of course. She used to go round to the farmer beside us and they used to give her milk for free, because she helped them out during busy times. And also we had to depend on the butcher's for all the cheap cuts we could get, because we had fifteen of a family. My grandmother had thirteen.

The men were the main breadwinners in the house, so they got the best food. The women thought it was better to keep the men warm and well fed, so that they could get to work. Now, coming to my time, I think there is more junk food, more fish and chips, more pastries and things like that, very unhealthy food. Grandmothers never believed in any of those things. It was all home baked. We never had to buy a loaf in those days. I never knew what a bought loaf was like. We are now more conscious of diet and health food and things like that.

Eileen, a Lurgan home help, recalled a similar diet.

The diet of our grandmothers was mainly porridge, potatoes, eggs, buttermilk, cabbage, home-baked bread,

51

bacon, fish, soup, stew, raw eggs beaten up in potatoes, pigs' trotters and tripe. The fruit diet was mainly apples, rhubarb, plums, blackberries and mushrooms. Most of these were in plentiful supply because they were grown locally. Mushrooms could be had by going out early in the mornings to the fields and picking them.

We found that the rural areas and the city were similar, because they had the same diet. Another thing which our grandmothers and our mothers did, they baked their own bread, soda and wheaten, apple bread, potato and rhubarb bread. At night, you got a boiled, a scrambled or a poached egg.

None of our grandmothers or mothers ever had a fridge. I got my first one twenty years ago.

Urban versus rural

Margaret, who lives near Lurgan, but whose family on one side lived in the country, felt country dwellers were better off; they had their own produce to eat or at least had more access to orchards and local crops.

City diets showed more variety, although the staples of the diet remained the same. City dwellers had the advantage over country people because the exporting and importing activities of the ports, especially at Belfast, had a spin-off in terms of good markets where people could buy a wider variety of foodstuffs.

A discussion by a group of women from Belfast resulted in the following report:

When we reflected on our grandmothers' and our mothers' diet, we felt that the food which was eaten was probably very much the same throughout and that it is really only in our time that the diet has changed quite a lot. They had root crops, cabbage, stews, soups and pigs' feet. They had winkles or willocks, which could be collected at the seaside or bought off sellers. Unemployed men would often go out to fishing ports or out to the country, and sell fish, herrings mostly, from handcarts. Or buckets of apples would be taken around. People went out blackberry picking, brought back the blackberries and made their own jam.

We talked about the food that would be eaten at feasts and holidays. Most of us remembered monkey nuts for Hallowe'en. These would be the cheapest kind of nuts. But there was nothing special other than that. Apples to some extent featured at Hallowe'en too. We weren't sure whether turkeys were particularly new or were quite a common thing to have had at Christmas time, or if the old idea of having geese was a part of the Christmas fare in the past. But everybody had stories about people's stockings being filled with fruit, apples and oranges. This proves fruit was a luxury. You got it for Christmas.

The importance of potatoes and bread in the diet is shown by the children's rhymes about the bread.

Barney Hughes' bread
It sticks to your belly like lead
Not a wonder, you fart like thunder
Barney Hughes' bread!

Commonplace foods had their own local names: elder (cow's udder), willocks (winkles), pigs' knobs (pigs' knees), a ticket of bread (four loaves together), golden drop (Indian meal). Cheap cuts and offal, pigs' feet, knee and cheek, ribs, elder and tripe, were important in the diet.

Officials who monitored public health in the early twentieth century noted that even in the countryside the staple diet of families would not amount to much more than bread and butter and cups of teas.

At times the food could be deadly. Belfast health authorities blamed the seafood eaten by city dwellers for outbreaks of typhus; it was gathered from the lough near sewage outlets and was bought at the door from street sellers. Typhus was the second major killer in the city, after tuberculosis.

Simplicity of the early days

Dietary patterns have obviously changed very much in recent times. Our recollections took us back to the simplicity of earlier times.

We discussed the distribution of food within the family. The man of the family would often get the best or maybe a different dish from the rest at the table.

Eating out is obviously a very recent thing, though there were eating houses for occasional treats in the past. People remembered going up the Shankill Road, and going into places where you could get stew and mushy peas. We talked about the importance of fish and chips as a regular part of food. Salads then would have been very plain. Offering food to visitors was important. It was the hospitable thing to do when people came into the house. But also if you were visiting you would bring something with you.

Treats were Paris buns and stomach cakes and bread with sugar. Buttermilk would be drunk regularly with meals. We remembered going out to get ice cream in a bowl. We talked about all the ice cream shops. All Italian shops, Morellis and Victors and Rossis, places that we remember as ice cream and chip shops.

If there was an old man living on his own or if the women lived near their parents and there was no longer anybody living at home, soup would be taken round. The bread delivery services, where bread was left on the sill, served as a kind of community sign. If the bread hadn't been lifted from the sill, it meant there was something wrong in the house.

We discussed the idea of cholesterol and whether cholesterol would have been a major concern in the past. Wholemeal and home baked bread and porridge and the whole foods that people are encouraged to eat now were central to the diet of earlier times.

We remembered the shops staying open on Saturday night; tick, buying food on the book and paying on a Friday night when the housekeeping money was handed over. Iris mentioned the bonus of living quite near the markets which provided varied food.

In Lent the frying pan would be hung up in Catholic districts. We recalled the Sunday morning fry. People would have gone to Mass, fasting, to take communion. Then when they came home they would have a big fry. This was the traditional Sunday morning breakfast.

Among the staples that women recalled was maize or Indian meal. In Derry it was introduced into the diet during the famine, and older people still call it golden drop.

Mention of the distribution of food within the family brought out one woman's story of the harsh price that women paid to feed other family members.

There was so little food about that my mother fed us, rather than herself. When she was hospitalised years later I was told that my mother's stomach had partly closed in. They said it was the result of malnutrition 'in her child bearing years'. I dare say that a lot of mothers of my mother's age had hard times. They fed their kids before they fed themselves. I thought that was very, very sad.

The change in diet came during the second world war. Women in the groups recalled ration books, dried eggs, Indian meal and spam, coupons and the long years when sweets were rationed.

The provision of school meals

One way that inadequate diets could have been improved was by the provision of school meals. Irish local authorities were slow to bring this in, despite public campaigns that began before the first world war.

It was well into the second half of this century before school meals were provided in all schools. Before that school meals came in at different times, depending on where you lived, and whether you went to a state or voluntary church-run school.

In Derry school meals were introduced in the 1950s and 1960s. Milk was introduced in the 1950s after the rationing, and was welcomed as a source of calcium. It helped to prevent rickets and TB, which were common at the time. School meals were very much welcomed. When they first came in they cost 2/6d (12 p) a week, and the unemployed got theirs free, which was a great boost, and nourished children who were deprived.

School meals were brought in around 1964 in Northern Ireland. Margaret recalled that families thought the school meals were the best thing that ever happened. Before that she would stand in the school yard and eat her packed lunch and was not allowed into the building to eat.

Not many of our group could remember exactly when school meals were introduced, except that they were at primary school (1950s and 1960s). School meals didn't mean much unless they were free. Many mothers couldn't afford to pay for school meals as well as meals at dinner time for the family. The milk was much appreciated. Unfortunately there was a stigma about school dinner tickets, because those who couldn't pay had to queue in a different line with a different colour dinner ticket.'

Mary can remember her teacher heating up the milk beside the school fire before giving it out to them. There were free school meals in St Kevin's school, but there was no dinner hall. The children had to cross a main road, and walk a few streets to a hall which belonged to the church. Milk was given out at 11 o'clock, from crates in each classroom. The children really looked forward to this.

The eating habits of the past, based on cheap, accessible, but

56

limited food, produced repetitious meals which hardly changed until recent decades.

Diet in the 'fifties

Kathleen and the women in her group recalled the food they themselves were given.

> *We found out most breakfasts were bread and jam, or bap and tea or porridge. There were really no cereals until you got older. They used margarine in those days. Stork and Echo margarine. Mary made butter for her granny by shaking a bottle of milk for hours.*
>
> *For your lunch, you'd have maybe leftovers from the dinner of the previous day. You got cabbage fried in the pan. And potatoes fried in the pan. You got turnip fried in the pan. You got bread and jam. Some put sugar on their bread. Some had dulse sandwiches. You might have wheaten bread, currant bread, and soda bannocks that were out of the bakery, nice and fresh. Sometimes Mary and Edie had scallops for lunch. There was pigs' trotters, pigs' feet, ducks' eggs and turkeys' eggs. We just have the one range of eggs now. There were a lot of different teas and a liquid coffee called Camp Coffee.*
>
> *For our dinners there was cabbage and bacon ribs, turnip and sausages, bacon and onions and soups and stews. Friday was a day when most of us didn't eat meat. We had champ and we had rice and sultanas. Chips were sold in newspapers. You would go out for your brother and sister and call them for their dinner: 'Mammy wants you'. Edie never got a shout. She got a wallop on the ear from her sister Mary. You didn't question your dinner, or say what you wanted. You just took what you got and were grateful for it.*

Kathleen has particular recollections of teatime:

There were so many of us there when we were having tea, my mammy used to make it in the big baking bowl. One by one you got your tea out of it in a tin mug. There were fifteen of us. There was no pot big enough for all of us, so it had to be the baking bowl, milk and sugar, the lot put into it. My mother made most of her own bread too, because in our house you couldn't have kept up with the demand for it. It was cheaper for my mother to make all the bread herself. Most people had fries on Saturdays. You had your dipped bread, so you had, and your sausages and bacon, and your eggs, soda farls and potato bread.

Saturday night the fireside soup was made. Most of our mothers spread out the newspaper and started to cut the vegetables, and soup was made for your father coming in at night. He got the bowl of soup. The peas for Sunday dinner were steeped overnight in the bowl. If you didn't eat your dinner, you got no jelly and custard, or rhubarb and custard.

For treats you bought gooseberries or picked blackberries. There were bullseyes, lucky bags, Paris buns and stomach cakes. Kamp apples were bought in buckets. A handcart came around and your ma went out to buy. There were humbugs, and sometimes you got a halfpenny or a penny in them. They were big humbugs, lemon or pink, with sugar on the top. When you got the penny you were able to go and buy another one.

Most people had a tickbook at the corner shop during the week and paid for everything at the end of the week. At Christmas the shopkeeper gave his regulars tins of biscuits. The shops sold bacon from big sides. You didn't get it prepacked. People bought butter from the block. Potatoes were sold from big sacks and weighed half-stones and quarter-stones. You never got the potatoes prepacked. You needed a basket to bring them home.

In discussions about religious dietary rules and fasting one woman joked, 'I don't think fish was only for Catholics. My mother cooked us Fenian steak every week.'

The changes in the food we eat today, in contrast to the earlier decades we looked at, was most marked by the variety of foods available and the wider range of places to eat it, whether at home, in restaurants, or in workplace canteens. In looking back we were reminded that today food itself has become one of the most debated concerns of public health.

Women and children, Raphael Street, Belfast, 1912.

Housing

Common privy at end of court, Millfield, Belfast.

Housing and conditions of housing have always been cited as an important contributor to health. So housing became one of our areas of interest in our Health and History project. We began with a discussion on the type of housing that families lived in at the turn of the century.

Anna, a school meals worker from Omagh, but born and reared in Glasgow, set the scene by reflecting on the different names of houses, which changed according to type and locality.

The different terms for houses are fascinating. Margaret's granny had what was called a kitchen house. Now that to me in Glasgow would have been a house with a kitchen only. But Margaret's grandmother in Belfast had a kitchen and two bedrooms.

In Glasgow I was reared in a room-kitchen on the third floor in a tenement building and I thought it was paradise up there. Kathleen, who lives in Co Tyrone, had what was called a one-bay house; it had one bedroom. And Eileen lived in a parlour house in Lurgan, and that had two bedrooms. Nice names.

The 1900s to the 1940s

Anne, a part-time worker in Coleraine, recalled domestic life based on overcrowding, few amenities and financial hardship, recognisable to rural and urban families alike in the first half of this century.

From the 1900s to the 1940s most of the houses were owned by gentry - landlords, mill owners, foundry owners. In the Coleraine area, especially, it was mostly foundry owners and farmers who owned houses. They hired workers and provided them with homes to live in. These were called tied houses.

63

Also there were half houses, where a family lived upstairs and a family lived downstairs; something like today's flat, one house and people living on two levels. And usually there were only about two rooms to a house, and maybe ten or eleven in a family. Three slept at the top of the bed, and three at the bottom of the bed. That was how they had to sleep.

And in those days they had two doors, one full door and a half door. They used to keep the top one open and sit and chat to the neighbours as they went up and down the street. The houses then had only bare floors, cement floors, wooden tables and that. But they were always kept white. Sparkling. Doorsteps and all.

There was no water or toilet or anything like that inside the house. It was all outside, and a bucket out in the backyard. On Saturday night water was brought in from the pumps, or the wells, whichever. This was bath night. Big pots of water were heated up and everybody in the family bathed. They had special clothes which they wore on Sundays only. And shoes, well they had only one pair of shoes. So anyone who lived in outlying areas of Coleraine would walk in their bare feet to the town, and put their shoes on at the outskirts of the town, before they came in.

The women were mostly in the home because as far as the men were concerned, if their wives were out working it didn't look good for them. The women usually boiled a big pot of spuds every day, and everybody had spuds for dinner.

And then in Belfast, the families were very close knit and they all married within their own area and their own religion, and they married around the age of twenty-five, which is later than today.

Anne's grandmother and her mother, Dora, who joined Anne in the project, had lived in tied housing.

Edie, a Belfast hospital worker, described her grandparents' home in the city, marked by overcrowding, but improved by her grandfather's talent for furniture making.

Our grandmothers all lived in small terraces, and they had large families, some of them. As large as sixteen. Sometimes parents and married children lived in the same house. Also my grandfather was very handy with his hands and made his own furniture. Years ago people just used wooden boxes for furniture. We had lovely marble tops on the dressing tables in our grandfather and grandmother's house.

Rita, who works with Edie, talks about the Belfast homes her grandparents knew.

Years ago, in my grandmother's time, there were many private landlords. And there were a lot of tied houses. There were two-up and two-down houses, and there were a lot of outside toilets. People took in lodgers and they took in other children. When people died, children were taken in. Marie's granny took in other children to help rear them. Unpaid for. It wasn't like fostering children today. And the landlords owned streets of houses. When people left, you had to pay key money to get the house for rent.

Another woman in the group recalled the tied housing.

Owners of mills built houses, and if you were put out of work, you were put out of your home as well. Our family saw this taking place.

Marie, a Belfast community worker, pointed out,

In Belfast the Conway mill built the houses in Conway Street, as did Rosses' mill in Rosses' Street. In Cavendish Street the houses belonged to Barney Hughes' flour mill and bakery.

Edie recalls how her mother in Belfast faced little improvement from her grandmother's day.

Small terraces again. One room accommodation. Some people with large families were able to merge two houses into one. Some also had outside toilets. People shared a wireless. We had stone-tiled floors, distempered walls, whitewashed yards, newspaper for toilet rolls. In our family the eldest child lived with our grandmother and looked after her. We had cold presses in the yard. They were wee boxes, with wire, that you kept the meat in.

Anne, a nurse from Derry, recalls the crowded housing in that city.

The dwellings in the city were terrace houses. When Dora's mother married, she moved to a farm where she lived in a tied house. If her husband lost his job, they lost their home. Her mother actually didn't get a decent house until she was dying, when they moved her out of a labourer's cottage into a fairly decent bungalow, to die.

Sarah's granny had eight of a family, and lived in a small terraced house. My granny had nine. Dora's granny had thirteen of a family, and Dora's mother had fifteen. Ann and myself had two each. We'd a bit of sense, you know.

Anna, who works in Omagh's school meal service, described her childhood home in Scotland, before the war, and gave a picture of the resources of Glasgow women, living in small, crowded homes without domestic amenities.

We lived in Springburn at the top of a tenement in Glasgow. There were three people on each landing and there was a shared toilet at the top of the landing. This was marvellous. There was newspaper toilet roll, which you cut up with the scissors with the fancy wee edges, pinking shears. We had electricity. We had no hot water, but we had cold water in the kitchen.

Like Eileen's mother, my mother would gather up our clothes, usually on a Monday, and go to the steamie. This was a fantastic place. You could wash clothes there and get them dried. In some steamies you were able to iron the clothes. When I was very young, she'd put me on top of the pram and off we'd go to the steamie. It was a social event as well. Women sang there. It was hard work, but they had hot water, washing boards and such like. They were doing it in an atmosphere where everybody else was in the same circumstances. The gossip was wonderful. You had a huge spin dryer that everybody put their clothes in and you had big drying horses which didn't take long to dry clothes as you sat and shared experiences.

Slow improvements of the 1950s

Anne, whose family have lived for generations in Co Derry, continues the story of housing at the end of the war.

In the 1940s the council started to build houses and prefabs, with electricity, and bathrooms. That's when they started to have oilcloth and that, rather than bare floors.

The first survey of Northern Ireland housing took place in 1943. It found 100,000 new homes were urgently needed and another 200,000 required to replace existing poor stock. War-time bombing had added to the crisis. This urgent target of 1943 was not reached until almost twenty years later.

Behind the surveys and statistics piled up years of neglect and harrowing housing conditions. Anne, a Belfast hospital worker, remembered those days.

We did a survey as young Christian workers in Belfast on the housing conditions and health. We found that Beechmount in the lower Falls had the highest percentage of TB in Belfast at the time, 1950. We also went to a house on the Crumlin Road and found that there were fifty-six people living in that one house. The scandal was brought out in the papers at the time. We went up to the top of the house, and an elderly man and his son were living there. We had been the first people to visit them and see what their conditions were like. He was an ex- soldier. He had two buckets and a basin to catch the water falling from the roof. I think at the time the rent was £1.10 a week. They didn't have the information or the knowledge to go and find out things for themselves.

A number of the women in the project had endured similar housing conditions themselves.

Eileen, a Lurgan home help, married and moved to her first house around 1957.

We couldn't use the bedroom because it was so damp and there were mice, so we all slept in the sitting room, or the kitchen as we called it. My husband and I and the children had to sleep where we lived during the day. We couldn't have used the bedroom because the water was coming off the walls, and when it rained you had to put out a big bath to catch the rain. So I was continuing on what my grandparents had. I lived in the same circumstances they had lived in for years. Later we moved and we had two bedrooms. There were eight of us and I had the luxury of being able to use the two rooms, although they were cold.

Anna came to live in Ireland in the 1950s. She recounts the Northern Ireland housing conditions told by women of the same generation as herself.

Now the improvements from the grannys' time to the mothers' time was that Margaret moved to a house in Milltown, where she had an outside toilet, which apparently she shared with a goat. It kept appearing for some strange reason! She enjoyed the luxury of a parlour and a living room. She moved then to a new house, with an inside toilet, and thankfully, no goat. That was about

1948. The drinking water was still drawn from a well. And it took four years to get the water inside the house. They had electricity and they had a huge garden.

So we come, then, to where we were all born, and where we are living now. Margaret was born in a kitchen house which had no electricity. Now she is living in a four bedroomed house, centrally heated, with her washing machine, fridge, television, microwave, and she has a lovely car, which, she will tell you, was bought with redundancy money. So the difference is quite remarkable.

Eileen, we found out, was born in Springburn, in Glasgow, where I was born. A small world indeed. Eileen can't remember too much about Springburn, but she can remember about Govan, where she lived.

Kathleen (in County Tyrone) was in a bay house, with no electricity or water. It had a dry toilet, which she or her mother emptied outside. I had to do that too when we went to our house in Omagh. To this day the smell of Jeyes fluid haunts me. Kathleen has moved from her one bay house. She has now got an Executive house with four bedrooms and two toilets.

The Derry nurse, Anne, recounts the story of the housing in that city.

I was reared in an estate in Derry called Creggan. It was a very new estate. My parents moved in after my mother had her first child. The reason for the change was because they had been living in a basement until then, in terrible conditions. And it was rat infested. This was about 1947 because it was before I was born. My mother got a councillor down to look at it. They had what you'd call a housing protest. I think it was the first of its kind, because a Labour MP, Major Bing, MP for Hornchurch, came over from England, and when he was in Ireland he saw my mother's home.

Today, although the housing situation isn't as bad in

Derry, I think the whole situation has done an about turn. It has become intolerable again, because of the high flats. They're knocking them down now. It was a ridiculous situation, because the lifts were always out of order. If you had someone with a heart attack at the top of the flats, the ambulance men had to walk up to bring them down. Or if you had a fire at the top of the flats, the firemen's ladder could only go so far, and they had to climb the rest of the way.

Housing protests of the 'sixties

As the slow pace of new and replacement housing dragged through the 1960s people's impatience mounted. The short supply of housing stock for the people meant allocations of housing were closely guarded by political interests.

Anna, from Omagh, describes the wave of housing protests that erupted at the poor conditions and sectarian allocations in the late 1960s.

We seemed to be fairly good at protesting about houses, or the lack of them.

In Dungannon, Kathleen was protesting around about 1969, against housing discrimination. She marched up and down for about three years. She eventually got a house in a mixed estate, alternate housing, catholic and protestant. It was a very good house. When intimidation started she had to pack up and move away from her home and go and live in an all catholic estate. And that probably was the start of the new ghettoes.

Eileen was protesting as well. She protested every year about flooding and eventually something was done.

Margaret had a tenants' association very early on in the 1950s.

I got my house around 1956. It was a fairly good house, but the amenities were quite bad. It was the way they built estates. We were stuck out there and there was

nothing for the youngsters to do. So we created a tenants'
association and campaigned for a community centre, and
were very successful. We got this smashing big community
centre. We were flabbergasted at first. Now there are six
in Omagh. We campaigned on things like bus services.
Before, you had to walk in and out of town. So we got a
bus service going, from all parts of the town, into different
parts of the estate. And basic things like a telephone box,
which we didn't have, but which was very necessary. That
tenants' association is still functioning. We have only the
one fireplace in our houses, and they are trying to get
central heating put in.

Anne remembers the start of Derry city's housing protests in
which her mother was closely involved.

In 1963 there were full three generations of people living
in Springtown camp in huts that the Americans used
during the war. When the Americans moved out, families
were moved in. The huts were really bad. TB was rife in
them and so was dysentry.

In 1963 my mother and twenty other people took over
the Derry Guild-hall and protested. She was a member of
the Labour Party. They were arrested, but the people were
rehoused. They were moved into Creggan, and
Springtown camp was knocked down.

Then in 1968, life was totally impossible, and I became
involved in the Derry Housing Association. We moved a
caravan into the middle of one of the main roads in Derry
and blocked it. The Derry Housing Association fought for
houses for people and we got accommodation bills
through. It then became political and directed towards
civil rights. There were two divides, the Nationalist party
and the Unionist party, and we were in the middle. And we
were 'communists', according to them, because we wanted
decent housing for people.

In our discussion group I was the only one who

71

became involved in housing protests. I was two years old when my mother went on her first protest. She dragged us along. Sarah's uncle was a councillor. He was labelled a 'communist' too. None of us, with the exception of Sarah's mother, was moved during the troubles.

Anna told of the struggle that women had to get decent housing.

Margaret applied to the council by way of a form and she lobbied the councillors. Kathleen got hers because of overcrowding. And she was overcrowded for a year, and then she got her form. But she had to torture the district office to get it. And Eileen likewise. She also approached the MPs. She tortured the MPs. So she got her house. I did the same. Took four years. Things move slowly in Omagh. We had to go around the councillors, and only to those of your own religion. If you wanted a house you had to go to a catholic councillor. You would be down on your knees begging. It just depended. It took me four years, but we got our house eventually.

1970s: The Payment of Debt Act

Anne, from Coleraine, took up the continuing story of housing from her group.

Then in the 1970s the (Housing) Executive came in. In earlier years the rent was paid to a man calling at your door, and then as time went on, you paid it into the post office. During this second period we had rent and rate strikes, and a lot of people got into debt. So they started to take it out of people's benefits and wages. People had no way of knowing about it, until they got their money and found so much deducted out of it to cover their debts.

This kind of thing happened very frequently. One particular person had £30 taken out of their wages in one week and only got £39. That was the Payment of Debt Act in operation.

The rent and rates strike began in 1971 in protest at the introduction of internment. The government's response was the Payment of Debt Act, by which outstanding local authority rents and rates were deducted from benefits and public sector wages. In time the Payment of Debt Act was used to reclaim personal debts for all public utilities as well as rents or rates. It has since been replaced.

Housing initiatives in the 'seventies

Redevelopment, which began in the 1960s, and the troubles in the 1970s, brought more housing changes, particularly in the cities.

Rita described these changes in Belfast from the 1960s.

People started trying to buy their own houses. There were a lot of changes. There were high rise flats, and an awful lot of young families went into them. And it must have been hard for them. People, maybe living six storeys up, with three or four children, and having to bring the prams up and down stairs.

My mother is seventy-four now. She lived in a two bedroomed house all along, and reared a big family. Now she has a three bedroomed house, for herself and just one boy.

We've better housing in some places. But at the start of the troubles, when people were put out of their houses or burnt out, they were moved into wooden chalets. People were left in them for too long, and weren't given any other accommodation, so they squatted in new houses that were being built. There were rats eating through the floorboards and dysentry and meningitis were common in these chalets.

Rita lost her own house in the 1970s in the troubles. It had cost her £1,500 and she had lived in it for twelve years, spending about £2,000 on it during that time. The same house today costs approximately £25,000. Now she is a Housing Executive tenant.

Anne, from Coleraine, described another housing initiative.

In 1978 co-ownership came up, which is where the government owns a percentage of your house. This is really a con because you have to buy it back, but you buy it back at the going rate, not at the rate for which you bought it. The homes were just plain, but they weren't as well-built as they were before. Now in the houses we have everything from tumble dryers and automatic washing machines to fridge freezers, whereas my mother used to do with the scrubbing board.

Modern housing conditions

Women summarised such dramatic changes by comparing the advantages and drawbacks to the earlier housing their families knew.

Anne, from Coleraine, recognised that people today own more than their mothers or grandmothers could ever have expected.

We did agree in our discussion that we had all these things, but that at the same time people went into a lot of debt to get them.

As we talked it was clear most of us felt that houses were more shoddily built and we noted that the new equipment and household gadgetry broke down all the time.

In the discussion on housing women remarked on how often it was the woman in a family who had the responsibility of searching out and applying for housing.

Anna considered the impact of housing clearance and the building of new towns to rehouse families from redevelopment areas in Belfast, in particular.

Families got separated. Before, you lived beside your granny. You went to work with your neighbours. That no longer happens. You've a daughter living over here, and a

74

son over there. Craigavon is a whole new town, purpose built to provide housing and employment.

Other women made the same points about the new towns.

People were asked to move to the likes of Craigavon and Antrim. And they were given a lump sum, but they had to stay in these houses for three years, or else repay the money. There was no employment locally, and the houses were badly built. A lot of these houses have had to be demolished.

Edie brought the discussion up to date on the housing problems in some of the new Belfast estates.

House improvements are carried out now since housing groups put pressure on the council. There's also a problem now with high rents. There are more houses in a smaller space, and there's joyriding and 'bow' (cider) drinking going on.

Rita summed up one of the most striking changes.

Now there are fewer people in the houses, because going back years ago, people had thirteen and fourteen children. But we've caught ourselves on now. And as for single people, you get an awful lot of young ones who leave home and buy their own houses. They're breaking out and buying houses even before they are married.

Woman doing her washing.

Women's work

Interior view of laundry showing women using steam irons.
Edgar House, 14 Brunswick Street, Belfast, 1900.

For women in the north of Ireland at the start of this century working lives began young. There was not a wide range of jobs for women. There was not a lot of work for anyone, but women, young women, could find employment more readily in the north than their sisters elsewhere in Ireland, or sometimes even, than their brothers in the same house.

Linen workers

These memories recount how young women found work in the textile and clothing industry of the north of Ireland's towns and cities. Linen, in Belfast alone, employed an estimated workforce of 50,000 women in the opening decade of this century, in both mill and factory, and among the army of women employed in their own homes at the finishing trades of thread drawing, hemming and embroidering.

The women in the project, all working in the public services of health and education, found they shared a common inheritance of grandmothers and often mothers who worked in the linen industry, most commonly, but not exclusively, as mill workers.

Mary, a Belfast hospital canteen worker, shared this family background of the early twentieth century.

When my grandmother was ten she was known as a half-timer. She went to Dunlewey Street school for three days and then had to work in the mill for three days. If she missed a day at school, she lost a day's pay. There was a mill on Campbell's Terrace and it had a school on top.

Margaret, a Craigavon nurse who was born in Belfast before her family moved out of the city, had a similar background.

My grandmother worked in the mill until she was seventy-three. My mother worked in the mill, and she went to school half-time. She worked from when she was about

79

twelve. You went to school and you worked the other half.

Margaret herself had started her working life in the linen industry.

My first job was in the bleaching works, a linen factory where they bleached the cloth. I was fourteen on a Sunday and I started work on the Monday. If they had opened on a Sunday I'd have probably had to go that day.

Child labour

Half-timers were children, usually from the age of twelve, (although these accounts show they could be even younger), who spent half of their time at school and half at work. In Ulster the six day working week, as Mary's account tells, was divided into three full days schooling and three days working. Commentators on the poor record of health in the north pointed out that the British system, which split each day in half, with school in the morning and work in the afternoons, was less onerous on the children and less damaging to their health.

Robert Lynd, a Belfast journalist, condemned the half-time system he knew in the city in 1909.

Vitality is slowly squeezed out of them, and it is hardly any exaggeration to say that from the age of fifteen upwards they die like flies.

When he wrote this Belfast had a reputation as an unhealthy place in which to live, with an abnormally high death-rate. The city fathers had set up an enquiry in 1907 to collect the age, gender and causes of death from the official registers, and compare these with other Irish and British cities.

The statistics left no room for complacency, although there was some relief that the enquiry found the death-rate was not excessive. In every age group under the age of fourty-five years, more women than men died in Belfast. Particularly vulnerable were women between the ages of ten and thirty-five years. The 'death-rate of women at child-bearing ages was considerably higher in Belfast', the report concluded.

Working conditions at the mill

Rosaleen, a Belfast hospital worker, recalled the conditions that gave rise to the city's devastating death toll among its young women, from the family memories of a group of Belfast women.

In the early 1900s all our grandmothers worked in the mills. Rita's granny and my granny were both half-timers. They were in school half the time and worked the rest, when they were about ten or eleven years old.

We found that jobs more or less passed from mother to daughter, and a family connection got you a job. My grandmother was a doffing mistress (an overseer of the bobbins on the spinning machine) in Greeve's mill. So obviously my mummy got a job and granny's sisters and their daughters got jobs. There was no problem.

As I say, there was great ease in getting jobs then. If people didn't like the mill they were in, or if they fell out with the foreman or something, they just got another job. They came in that afternoon, handed in their notice, and maybe started another job the following morning. Up until the 1920s that was really the only type of work available. Most of the women worked at the mills.

There weren't any health or safety regulations. Most of the women who that worked in the mill had very bad feet, because they stood in water all the time. They had leg ailments because of the time they had to spend standing. And they had very bad chests because of the pouce* that was in the air. There were people who had 'pouce chests' because their complaint came from the stuff that came off the flax.

But believe it or not, one of the good things was, you could always have told a mill worker by the skin on her hands and feet and face. They always had beautiful skin.

* *Pouce*, used in Scotland as well as in Northern Ireland is the airborne lint that came off the spinning thread.

*They started about six o'clock in the morning. It was a
long day. They worked from six in the morning to six at
night. Marie recalled that when they came out of the mill
at six at night they used to come down the street in droves,
hundreds of them, singing.*

If they survived the rigours of the mill, grandmothers often
lived long working lives. Margaret's grandmother worked in the
mill until she was seventy-three. Eileen, a home help from
Lurgan, had a grandmother with a similarly long working life.

*My grandmother worked until she was eighty. She quit the
winding of cloth in a linen factory when she was seventy-
five. Then for the rest of the time she did housekeeping
down at McDaid's. You know McDaid's, down Edward
Street? She took the old man's washing home until she was
eighty-one.*

Rural work

Linen threaded its way through the small towns of the north of
Ireland. Kathleen from Co Tyrone outlined the working lives of
three generations of women in her maternal family, starting with
her grandmother.

*Farming, that's what she did. My mother then worked in a
mill. I worked in the mill at the start and then at the
hospital.*

Her grandparents had lived on a family-owned farm typical of
agricultural holdings in the north of Ireland.

*Well, my grandparents owned a bit of land. He worked for
the council, and she kept the bits and pieces running, you
know. I only know about the one grandmother.*

Margaret recalled an episode of rural life two generations
past.

My husband had a very interesting grandmother. That's

the one who couldn't read or write. They had cows, and she sold milk. She supplied milk to one particular man who was well off and could afford to pay for it. But he didn't pay. She had dotted down on the barn door, just chalk marks, all the times he didn't pay. And she took him to court, and they took the barn door to the court to show the judge how much he owed her!

I don't know much about my husband's grandmother, other than, you know, she had a grave out in the cemetery, and if any local children died around her and if they couldn't afford graves for them, they were all buried in my grandmother's grave.

Rural work for women often meant a more casual form of employment, earning a living from particular tasks and seasonal work.

Dora's family have lived within the same district for three generations at least. Her family history is told by her daughter, Anne, who shared in her mother's family recollections.

Dora's grandmother was a farm labourer. Before she was a farm labourer she collected scollops. She went into town and sold them for 2/6d at the town centre, to try and keep her family; this was her only income.

Questioned by the younger listeners, unfamiliar with the term 'scollops', Dora explained:

Remember the old thatched cottages? Well, scollops were used to pin down the thatch to the roof. Scollops were made from briars. People would go round the hedges, scour them and clean the jags off them. They would then put them into bundles of twelve, take them down to the Diamond at Coleraine, and sell them to the farmers for thatched roofs.

Dora's granny, Anne added, 'was put out to the hiring fairs as a farm labourer'. This was the only direct experience of the hiring fairs amongst the personal histories of the project. Yet they had been part of rural life in Ireland right up to the war. Once or twice a year in the country towns young men and women went to fairs to be hired to the wealthier farmers, who bought their labour for a set period of the farming year, paying them, or their families, an agreed price. The hired servants or labourers got bed and board for their contract, though this was customarily provided in an outhouse.

In Derry women found work most commonly in the shirt industry. It was the largest industry in the city, but none of the Derry women had grandmothers who worked in it. It was in the next generation, their mother's age group, that the women of these families took up their work in shirt making.

The depression of the 'thirties

An economic crisis took root in Northern Ireland in 1921, as traditional industries of shipbuilding and linen foundered in the slump after the first world war, and never recovered. When the depression came ten years later the crisis deepened.

Mary, a canteen supervisor from Belfast, told her grandmother's story of seeking work in the depression.

In the hungry 'thirties my grandmother had to travel to different mills. She lived on the Falls, and she travelled as far as Dunmurray and Greencastle. She had to catch the tram at five in the morning.

People out of work in those years had to turn to the poor law receiving officer for discretionary payments based on a family means test, paid out to the able-bodied unemployed. Outdoor relief, as these payments were known, ensured the privilege of living at home and not being forced into the workhouse.

The begrudging way these payments were made, the insistence that families must sell every small item from their home before relief was given and the ever present threat of work schemes led to growing protests and serious rioting in Belfast in October, 1932. Newspaper photographs show how much of the hardship devolved on women family members, who queued with their children at the doors to receive relief.

Wartime work

Changes in women's work came with the war, not because industrial or agricultural work changed dramatically, but because in most families women, and men, went away to work.

Rosaleen told the Belfast memories of the impact of wartime.

Marie recalled that her aunt Chrissie worked in a munitions factory in London. Some of the women went away to work there. My own father went. Well, he was in the army during the war. A lot of men went to London. They went because there was no work here. Marie's granny actually worked for the American Red Cross.

Two women in the project had mothers who had done non-traditional work. Both had grown up in Scotland, unknown to each other, and both mothers had taken up work in the war-time munitions industry.

Eileen tells her mother's story.

She worked in the munitions during the war. Up the Langholm Road in Govan, in the rope works. A big, big red brick building, down the whole road. She then went to England and they had two shops, vegetable shops, and she worked till she was seventy-five.

Anna, recounting the life cycle of her mother's work, told a similar experience.

I'm not sure what my granny did. Now my mother worked in J and P Coates' mill in Paisley in Scotland; they manufactured spools of thread. She was a winder on to the bobbins and she had to work with her toes as well as her hands. She had to work on stone floors. There were pretty horrendous conditions in that mill. It's still there, but now it's a hotel. The other one is derelict.

After she got married she didn't work in the mill any

more. She worked for other people just cleaning houses. Then along came the war, and my father went to join up. And she went along to Bairdmore in Springburn, which was an extremely large munitions factory. She was a woman who could've tried anything. She ended up driving a crane, and she took great pride in being a crane driver, lifting things along. This was a man's job and she thought it was great. Very, very long hours. But she loved it.

Then the war was over, back came her husband and off she went, back into doing housework for other people, a job which she detested. Her last job was cleaning offices in a garage at night.

Cheap labour

The working lives of the women today were usually much more varied than their grandmothers'. Many, in Margaret's words, words, had 'flitted around to where the best money was'. Such varied careers also reflected changes in job opportunities. The collapse of the linen industry meant work had to be found in other jobs and trades. Marriage and having children inevitably led to changes in jobs and time out of the workforce.

Dora was very young when she began her working life in the countryside just after the war.

Dora worked as a farm labourer as well as going to school, from the time she was twelve years old. When she left school she looked after her granny until she died. Dora then got married, and started working as a press operator. She left to have her first baby. She went back to work at the same firm as a part-time cleaner.

Her next job was working as a railway attendant. She worked twenty-two hours a day. The first train running to Belfast was at 6.00 am, and there were goods trains running along the lines at 12 noon, 2.00 am, 3.00 am and 4.00 am. She had to stand in freezing cold weather, whilst these very long trains went through the gate. She only slept from 4.00 am to 6.00 am. With the job she was given a gate-house, which had only a dry toilet, no running water or electricity, no bathroom and two damp bedrooms. When she was working, a telephone was the only connection with the station. Dora remembers one terrible incident. The signal came up but there was no train due. She was in the process of opening the gate when the train flew through, hitting the gate and herself, almost killing her and causing severe damage to her foot. She was off work for some time. She was allowed to keep the cottage, but didn't get paid. The railway took on a schoolboy in her place and paid him less. Her employers told her it was her fault, for not hearing the bell.

She moved to another gate-house, which was slightly better, with running water, flush toilet, electricity and two bedrooms. She finished this job in 1972, for another on the railways as a crossing keeper. The hours were slightly better, 6.00 am to midnight, working a sixty to seventy hour week for £3.50. Dora then left the railways and started working as a part-time cleaner.

In the 1980's the Equal Opportunities Commission investigated the pay and conditions of crossing keepers like Dora, in cottages scattered along the Northern Ireland railway tracks, they found the employer called these 'cheap woman crossings'. Northern Ireland railways paid out tens of thousands of pounds to women in recompense of years of low pay when the women succeeded in an equal pay claim. The award virtually wiped out the company profit for that year.

Sarah, a canteen domestic from Derry, first worked in a shirt factory and left work for five years, when she returned as a part-timer.

Pressures of the job

Rosaleen traces similar experiences among the women she talked to, about their family work history.

We found there were mill workers, shirt factory workers, or stitchers as we called them. The mother of one of the

87

girls worked as a secretary. Marie's granny then started as a cleaner in the health service. Both Rita and I worked as stitchers. The place Rita worked in had the Tailor and Garment Workers' Union. They didn't have a union in the place I worked. We weren't allowed to be unionised. When a guy came around to try and unionise he was just chucked off the premises. There was no way they were letting the union in.

Workers often got their fingers caught in the sewing machine. You were lucky if the needle broke off. Most times it did. They sent you around to the mechanic and he just hauled it out with a pair of pliers. You ran your finger under water and stuck a plaster on and you were settled back at your machine. So that was their idea of health and safety.

It was still very easy to move from job to job and people never thought of job satisfaction. They went to work for the money, because they needed the money to eat.

There were a lot of controls in the factories. In the first one where I worked we had to ask for permission to go to the loo. We were only out of school and considered too young to speak up for ourselves.

People never thought then of women being trained for jobs. You couldn't walk off the streets into a mill and start being a doffer, a weaver or a spinner. They had to be trained, so they trained themselves. They treated a lot of their ailments themselves too. Nobody ever thought they were doing a job they had to be trained for. Even when you went into a factory to do shirts, or pillowcases, it was off the street, and use a wee sewing machine and make up wee trousers or dresses or whatever it was; you had to train yourself to do that.

In the 1980s people were under pressure. The only pressure earlier on was going to your day's work and coming back. Now people are losing their jobs. Losing the *means of making money is the greatest pressure anyone has. There is no such thing now as working for pin money.*

Part-time workers are usually four to six hours on their feet. In the public service, people have no option now but to stay in the same job. There is never ever any suggestion that women could be trained to move up the structures.

Job security is constantly under threat now. One young woman who works in administration is in the same position as those in ancillary and support services. She knows there is something going on. She says her immediate bosses are going around with their faces tripping them, but won't tell the workers anything. She doesn't know whether her job's under threat or not. At least if you know your job's going, you can get up and fight for it.

And home to domestic chores

There was little time for leisure in the past. But we explored what labour saving devices our grandmothers and mothers had, and what opportunities there were for breaks or holidays.

The resourcefulness of women was demonstrated by the stories recounted in group discussions. Many homes had a treadle sewing machine, which was updated as the technology became more sophisticated. But there was no relief from most heavy domestic chores. These remained women's responsibility, and all too often mirrored the work they were paid for outside the home.

Margaret, who had said her grandmother had left work when she started her family, corrected herself quickly, 'Her work was really only beginning.'

Eileen remembered wash-days every Monday and Wednesday in a house her mother cleaned.

She had to boil two huge kettles on an open grate. The people she worked for were fairly well off. She had to do the washing in the outhouse. She was not allowed to use the kitchen, so she had to carry large kettles to the

89

outhouse to do all the family washing, and then carry out the buckets to rinse. She had to wring by hand, and hang out the clothes on the washing line. On Tuesdays she did ironing. She earned two shillings an hour. Slave labour. She went home every day sweating and exhausted. Sometimes she cried herself to sleep with exhaustion. It was a hard life.

So it was at home too. Many of the women from the country recalled that their mothers had to draw water from a well. Their mothers' domestic luxuries in terms of labour saving equipment were running water, or electricity, or even, as in Kathleen's Tyrone family, a washboard.

Rita remembers, in Belfast, sometime in the 1950s, a man used to come around in a van, with a mobile washing machine, which he hired out for the day at five shillings a time. The launderettes of the 1960s were seen to be a great innovation for women with a busy household, faced with the family wash.

Holidays were rare, infrequent or unknown. Eileen's grandmother used to take a day out at the seaside, at Bangor or Warrenpoint, resorts that had become more accessible with the railways. Such day trips or bus runs were organised through the tiddly clubs. We recalled the history of the tiddlies from the mills right down to the present. In these informal saving clubs, women put aside a set, small, weekly sum from their wages. Traditionally, this money was used to pay for a charabanc and the expenses of a day out to the country or the seaside.

Today women keep up the practice in clubs, where weekly savings by a group of women at work are put aside for any young woman getting married. In other uses of this saving scheme, women pay in each week for, say, twenty weeks, after which each woman gets the full payout. Similar clubs collect for Christmas expenses. Clubs which gather savings to be given as a gift to a woman having a baby are known as 'sunshine clubs'. From all corners of the room in our discussions, women came up with their own variants on their grandmothers' tiddlies.

There were other ways of taking a break, without saving for it. Rosaleen told of the working holidays that families took in the

1950s and into the 1960s. A woman took a cottage at the seaside. The husband would stay in town and continue working, perhaps joining the family for a weekend. Children helped out working for local farmers or took seasonal jobs.

This pattern changed only in the 1960s. Butlins, rented caravan holidays, and trips to the Isle of Man became more frequent. Families had gone to the same place, the same time, year after year. The most recent change has been for foreign holidays, leaving the country for trips to the sun.

Entertainment was always modest. Grandmothers entertained in the home. Margaret and Kathleen recalled that weddings, wakes and churches played a significant part in women's social lives.

Outings were to the music hall, never to the pub. In the home women did not drink. The main excitement of the night would be the ghost stories.

One group of Belfast women tracing entertainments of the past were delighted to find that, no matter where they came from in the city, the same stories had reached them across generations of story-telling.

The 1940s especially brought the GIs and the ballrooms, and the odd trip to the pictures, to be replaced by TV, videos and bingo in the following years.

Belfast women remembered the Blouse Club, an exclusively women's club in the 1950s and '60s in the city.

Belfast Hospital for Sick Children, waiting room.

Knowledge of sex

A young woman in the north of Ireland was more likely to marry earlier than her sister elsewhere. A larger young population in the northern towns is a testimony of their large families. Ignorance about birth control seemed a universal experience of family life. Family memories testify that this lack of knowledge extended to sex itself.

We were clear that there was no knowledge of sex or contraception as far as our grannies, mothers or ourselves were concerned, until the 1960s or 1970s.

Our grandmothers learned nothing about sex from their mothers before they were married. We wondered what life was like for them.

Our grandmothers had no idea about contraception at all, or about the functioning of their own bodies. Neither did our mothers.

Sex was such a taboo subject that little of the thoughts, ideas or information which women had, or took recourse to, has survived in their granddaughters' memories. The silence between the generations is almost complete.

Fear of sex

There was only speculation by grandchildren on what emotions may have governed women in the 1900s.

Sex as a method of reproduction meant that women had a fear of sex. The fear was related to becoming pregnant; the end product was a child and they couldn't afford the child. So sex was always tinged with this fear: for five, ten or fifteen minutes' pleasure, you were going to end up paying for the rest of your life.

*The other fear that came from sex was of not knowing
anything about our bodies, or our bodily functions. The
whole fear of the unknown. The emphasis on reproduction
way back, when there wasn't any contraception, made
women, particularly women who were extremely fertile,
really worried. That gave rise to the saying, 'He has only
to look at her sideways, and she'll get pregnant.'*

*Helen works with old people, and she said it has
happened on a number of occasions that old women in
their seventies and eighties, because they know they are
near death, get very upset and ask to see a priest. When
questioned about why this is so important and urgent, they
say, 'It's because there's something I did wrong sometime
ago and I want to get it off my chest.' And it's basically
because they had a relationship that was not the norm,
given the codes of conduct and everything else. And
they've carried the memory along with them all these
years and felt guilty about it.*

A law for the rich, another for the poor

The speculation and the hints that came down through the years
led to some research among our groups. Why were richer
families small and the poorer ones large, we asked.

Encyclopedia Britannica provided some of the answers.
There women learnt that methods of birth control had existed
from the earliest times, from those used by the Egyptians to the
much more recent and merchandised methods, the condom
(eighteenth century) and the Dutch cup (nineteenth century).
Contraceptive methods had been available, this research showed,
for those who had access to the information and the money to
buy them. Sex campaigners for birth control were actively
propagandising 200 years ago. But their message reached only a
small number of women or men.

Abortion

Abortion had been illegal from 1861 but this has not stopped
women seeking ways of ending an unwanted pregnancy. Such
attempted abortions were usually self-induced. Rather than

women searching out an abortionist, as Kathleen, a Belfast home help recounts, they thought if they had baths, or took gin, they could do away with a baby. Or if they could jump from a chair, instead of stepping down, they would lose the baby.

Other methods of abortion were used, although these usually only came to public notice in court cases. We found a newspaper story of a Belfast chemist being tried for the death of a young woman in the city whom he had provided with drugs. Her boyfriend was tried, with the chemist, for procuring the illegal abortion for her. Witnesses came from as far away as Coventry in England to testify that this abortion practitioner's clients lived far beyond the city boundaries.

Marie was told by her grandmother that the handywoman in Tiger's Bay was known as an abortionist among the young women of her day.

In the early '60s a woman a couple of streets away from me got five years because through an illegal abortion a girl died.

One woman reported that her mother had once tried to abort. She used a variety of methods. One was eating washing soda.

A more desperate way of dealing with an unwanted child came to light in a small newspaper item, only weeks after the trial of the north Belfast chemist. A young woman living in the west of the city was on trial for having abandoned her new born baby to die.

Silence

The lack of knowledge we had from our grandmothers' days was repeated when our discussions reached our mothers' generation.

Only Margaret had learned from her mother that women who did not get want to get pregnant had used a douche, 'to get rid of the man's sperm'. All the other women reported that their mothers had never known of any means of birth control.

None of us learned anything from our parents about sex. We had to rely on outside influences, which today includes the media.

Some women did not know anything about what happened during sex until it happened. One woman said that when she went into hospital she thought the baby would come out of her belly button.

Another woman explained that the imposed silence between the generations of her family was mutual.

You did not talk to your mother about it. Even if you were married you did not talk about it, because she never told you anything about pregnancy or sex. My mother came and told me, 'For God's sake, do not get pregnant. Not any more.' I was three months pregnant at the time. She didn't find out until she was told that she had another granddaughter. I couldn't tell her. I was too embarrassed.

Schooling did not provide us with any alternative route to knowledge. Sex education in the secondary schools of the 1960s was usually given by a teacher, but was not part of an integrated school curriculum. Most women who were given sex education at school had it presented as a once-off event in the form of a booklet, a film and a talk. Family reaction to such initiatives could be mixed.

I was sent home with a wee book. My mother hit the roof and went to see the nun. The nun was called everything.

When it came to the time of the film and the talk, it was, 'You are not allowed to see it.' I was glad because they were all sick coming out of it.

Some of the women were taught by nuns, who had a peculiar idea of sex. Even in the mid-'60s sex was not discussed in schools run by nuns. Marie remembers one nun saying that, when you went out with boys, you were not to wear 'black patent shoes because they reflect your knickers'. One other old story was that if you sat on a boy's knee, you had to put a 'phone book below you, so that flesh never touched flesh.

Now sex education has become more available, assisted by access to TV and radio.

There's great knowledge of sex among younger people today, but not enough knowledge of their own bodies. Sex education is a lot better at school, but still not adequate.

Children today find out before their parents tell them, because of sex education. Children now could educate their parents about sex.

Sex education in schools today is making children more aware of sex in general, at an early age.

Folklore and myth

In the almost total absence of information and education about women's health and well-being, folklore and myth is widespread. The onset of periods was a time of prohibition and confusion for young girls.

Don't wash your hair. Don't swim. Don't wash your feet. Don't do PE. Don't let boys near you. Women are still quite vague about the whole gynaecological system of their own bodies. Apart from Marie, none of the women in the group knew what periods were until they started; they had not been forewarned about such things. As a girl, Margaret thought that they only happened once in your life. Anne thought that if you ate a coloured pea you got pregnant.

One woman remembered her mother telling her that if she washed her hair, she would end up like the woman around the corner who had a mental defect. Iris had fallen at a horror film before she had her first period. She thought that the fall had caused the blood. Rita remembers a priest giving her a book about her periods. Kathleen thought that periods were necessary to get rid of pints of old blood, to be replaced by new blood.

Mary was told not to wash her hair or her feet when she had her period. Margaret's mother gave her a piece of

99

old sheet when she had hers without forewarning. Most of the women were told not to go near boys. Anne's mother told her not to play with boys any more. She began her periods very young, when she was nine years old.

There was quite a myth about tampons until quite recently. People thought you weren't a virgin if you used them. Marie's mum was shocked when she saw her using them. Anne's doctor still believes they are dangerous because they don't let the blood flow naturally.

Charting the history of women's sexuality through family memories we came up against the same obstacles of silence, ignorance and fear in our own generation.

Marie gave the background and conclusions of one group of women.

We started talking about where people actually learned about sex. Sex education was non-existent in schools until the last ten or fifteen years. But until then we still depended for our sexual education from our peer groups, either in the work place, in school or among our friends. The one thing that holds true, right through from the 1900s to the present day, is that sex is still not being taught in the home. It is not coming from parents. That highlights the dilemma regarding the public debate about whether sex education should be continued in the school or carried out in the family.

The fate of the victims

Marie extended the discussion to include the social stigma of illegitimacy.

We talked a bit about illegitimacy and the change in attitudes towards illegitimacy. Some of us felt that before, illegitimacy always carried a kind of stigma with it, for the mother and illegitimate child. Attitudes have changed very much, though there is a certain underlying element of hostility towards single mothers. But because there is so

100

much illegitimacy, and so many single mothers, the stigma's gradually gone down. We see that public figures, like rock stars and TV AM presenters, are getting pregnant and are not married, and, 'This is cool, sister'. I am not bringing it down. It is taking away the stigma that was there. Because these famous people have big incomes, they don't have to worry about it.

Amongst family memories were recollections of the fate of mothers and children outside the bond of marriage. Sometimes these had been close family members. In every story the solutions that were found to unwanted pregnancy were drastic.

Lily's aunt, who got pregnant at twenty, disappeared, never to be seen again. Cathy's sister was too terrified to let anyone know. She cleared off.

Another woman told how her aunt had gone missing because she was pregnant, and never came back again. Since they shared the same name, this woman had imagined that she was the child of her missing aunt, whenever she was in a childhood conflict with her own mother.

Women recalled strong community stigmas against single mothers, even when these were not family members.

I know a girl who was put into a mental home by her parents because she became pregnant. We reckon there are women in mental homes today whose only crime was getting pregnant.

A wee boy died in the 1960s. His mother had put him in with the chickens. She didn't want anyone to know she had got pregnant. She went to jail. God love her, she got six or seven years.

Lack of access to birth control

Just after the second world war, in preparation for the sweeping changes being brought into Northern Ireland as part of the new National Health Service, the Tyrone County Medical Officer report commented on how little birth control was used.

It is extremely interesting to note how slight has been the variation of the birth rate during the past five years. This is probably due to the fact that a considerable proportion of the population is precluded from the practice of birth control by reasons of religious scruples.

But lack of knowledge about where to turn for information was the main problem.

Lily from Omagh and Cathy from Belfast did not realise the existence of family planning clinics until the late 1970s. These might have been there before, but women didn't use them because of embarrassment. That's changing now, and everyone goes along to the family planning clinic.

Because Eileen lived in such a small rural area, she had never heard of contraception, in the 1950s. Even her friends wouldn't talk. Margaret recalled a book from which she got her sex education when she was married.

Religion had something to do with it. Again, the catholic church did not want anything to do with contraception. My recollection was that only after the catholic church heard of the pill, did they start talking about it.

Marie reported that if anyone had a catholic GP, it was impossible to go and ask for contraception. So most people used family planning clinics, because more advice was available there and contraceptives could be bought at the clinics; you didn't have to go to the chemists.

Two women learnt about contraceptives when they started their nurses' training. Another woman learnt from magazines.

The women discussed different methods of contraception, and they all agreed durex was quite off-

*putting. One woman said her husband thinks they are like
'eating dinner with gloves on'. A lot of women agreed that
sex is over-rated. In the past sex was regarded more as a
duty. Now women have more control over their own
bodies, and find they can say no when they want to.
Women can enjoy sex more now.*

Without family planning clinics, and so little access to public
information there were problems about finding means of birth
control.

*When buying condoms in the chemists, Margaret
remembers having to ask for tomatoes. Then the
pharmacist would wrap them up behind the counter, so
that no one could see. When she lived in England for a few
years, she couldn't believe her eyes when she saw a poster
on the wall in the grocers advertising cut-price durex.*

*We talked about the 1960s, when the real change
occurred in sexual activities with the pill, and women
were saying yes to everything and anything. And what is
happening in the 'seventies and 'eighties is that women are
defining what yes is. What kind of yes. Yes to what exactly.
The 'sixties did not show anything. It was yes to
promiscuity, if you like, but women weren't gaining
anything from that. They were just getting passed from
pillar to post, maybe having an orgasm along the way, if
they were lucky. But at the end of the day they were not
getting anything from it.*

Modern methods of contraception

The availability of the pill was viewed as a breakthrough in birth
control.

My mother wanted to use the pill, but the pope said no.

*Amongst the women in our group, different types of
birth control were used, from nothing, due to religious
teaching and moral objections, to the use of the pill, coil
and condoms. The pattern generally was, after having two
children, most women in the group went on the pill.*

103

Anna had four children before she went on the pill. Before that no doctor would provide it. When she brought home a year's supply, her mother-in-law found it and destroyed it. She then went out and got sterilised.

Sterilisation was a difficult option to pursue because many women found obstacles in following their choice.

One woman's sister had four children and her doctor advised her to be sterilised because she had problems every time she became pregnant. She was about to agree, but had to have the form signed by her husband. Her husband said no, because if he died she might want to have children by another man. She never did get sterilised, and now she has two more children. It is impossible to get sterilised without a husband's signature. It used to be the doctor's right on medical grounds. Now that right is taken away. The women agreed it was unfair that a woman had to have her husband's signature to be sterilised, yet a man did not have to have his wife's signature for a vasectomy. Also there is an age limit for sterilisation. Usually, you are not allowed to be sterilised if you are under thirty, except for health reasons.

Lasting impressions

Woman drawing water from outside water pump.

Several of the women who have contributed to this book have been involved in the project since its earliest days. We first took part in what one woman described as 'a novelty exercise' and stayed to nurture and encourage it into a primary means of awakening women in our union about their own value.

Some of the material could have been seen as sensitive, but we never encountered resistance from women divulging personal family history details, even though there emerged a few 'skeletons in the cupboard' in the process. There were a number of reasons for women's co-operation and participation, not least of which was the 'crack' involved. Memories of almost every workshop activity are coloured by the sight of women laughing, and applauding loudly when report-backs were called for.

As information began to flow within the workshops, the delight of the participants became obvious. One woman remarked, 'I began to realise that I knew about something important, about history, and I hadn't known I knew so much.' Another remembered it as a discovery of strength. 'Our history wasn't dry from a book. It was about real people, women like me. It made me feel a full person.'

The discovery that each of us was not only able to contribute, but was expertly qualified to do so, was a powerful new force that became the engine for our activity. Something else became more clear to us also, encouraging all the women to co-operate. One participant explained, 'It was like a jigsaw puzzle. Each one of us had a piece and we could make the whole picture only if everyone gave their piece.'

Revealing what had earlier been regarded as shameful or embarrassing about women in our families was made easy by the historical context in which it was set. Thus, we could talk easily about poverty, debt, hardship and sexual naïvety because there was now a record of the existence of such difficulties throughout the generations.

Amongst ourselves we could begin to trust the existence of the same problems in our own lives, because we learned that those difficulties were not to be borne as a personal stigma, but were the historical condition of many women. 'It was fascinating to watch the spaces fill up. The more writing on the charts, the more women were giving of themselves.'

Perhaps too, there was an element of perceiving ourselves to be like pioneers, uncovering the lives of the women that time forgot, women whose existence was integral to our own because they belonged to us, through blood ties and social relationships. The sense of initiating something of our own, recording uncharted knowledge, gave us a freedom that one woman described as having, 'No right or wrong answers. No test to pass at the end of it. We decided what questions had to be asked, and we found out the answers.'

Some of the women who began the project spoke about the changes brought about in themselves and in their views of one another, through working together and listening to each other. 'When I first met X, I really, really didn't like her. I thought she was ... well, I couldn't get on with her. She was just so different from me. But when she got into the history project and started telling all those stories about her granny, and living in the country, well, listening to each other's background helped us to accept one another and understand where we came from. Now look at the two of us. Pals for life. But she can still be a real pain!'

It was not only individual women who began to understand one another; sometimes the acknowledgement of someone else had much wider implications. At a workshop which NUPE women conducted at a large feminist conference in the 1980s we had our first example of discovering women's lives not only within the context of class or community, but also of race.

There was a travelling woman in our group and when she was filling in the chart, she was explaining the importance of her family's ways, and travelling people's culture. There was I, who never had a good word to say about them, and when this woman did her family's background, I really

108

began to understand how they fought to survive, because
we treated them like a Third World people.

A woman involved in the history workshop felt strongly that although it was an exercise we could do alone by investigating our own family history and those of neighbours and friends, it was only together that it really worked.

When we were working in groups, one person's
reminiscence would trigger off a memory in someone else
and another person might then explain how she knew
about a subject. It was like as if doors kept opening up,
one after another and we kept blowing the cobwebs away.
Like dusting off our own history.

Learning the lessons

Our ever increasing familiarity with the social conditions of the women in past generations led us to examine our own responses to present social and economic influences and to compare the areas of which we now have knowledge. This activity generated as much discussion and excitement as the history we had uncovered.

Looking at the extended family network, we had ample evidence of it serving as a bulwark against the onslaught of much of the worst social deprivation of the past. It provided an essential pool of child carers for women who were often the main breadwinners, and in many cases ensured that at least some practical needs were taken care of for elderly relatives who were no longer able to look after themselves. Such services were almost always undertaken by female family members. The females of an extended family provided another informal resource - one of experience and know-how for those just beginning the rigours of adulthood.

Nevertheless the control exerted on individual family members could be merciless, particularly in cases of women within the family who fell foul of its strict moral codes. We discovered several forgotten aunties, women who had offended the family's sensibility by having relationships which were disapproved of and/or bringing the shame of an unmarried pregnancy to the family. Some of these women were forced out from the family's protection and both the woman and her child alienated and disowned.

One activity repeated in many of our family backgrounds was a kind of latter day surrogacy, or as one of the participants called it 'sharing out the youngsters'. Very often couples with large families would have a child reared by its grandparents, or a spinster aunt ('to keep her company'). Sometimes neighbours who had the room and the means, 'adopted' one of the children from another family. Most commonly amongst our own group, it was grandparents who alleviated the pressure of too many children in the family by taking responsibility for the rearing of one of them. This practice is still prevalent in many working class areas and may even be on the increase, because despite common and valid explanations of providing comfort and company to aging relatives, it tends to be a social indicator of declining economic resources.

The acknowledgement of this trend provided us with a new perspective on the recent debate regarding the right of grandparents to adopt their grandchildren in circumstances where the parental presence is not available or adequate. The long prevailing custom of grandparents providing a home for their grandchildren has not had public recognition.

It was most frequently in the section we called 'old wives' tales' that we found examples of past practices which have relevancy and practical application for present day use. Remedies and warnings, dismissed as 'the superstitions of old women', are now being proven by modern medicine to be based on sound diagnosis and prophylaxis. There are still remedies which defy any attempt at explanation. The passing of a child, suffering from whooping cough, three times under a donkey continues to baffle us, but no doubt was more baffling for the donkey concerned!

Abortion now, as in the past, is not an easy topic for women. The women in the Health and History project felt no more comfortable with it than most others. As a group we are a fairly balanced cross section of ages and experiences, bound together by our work in the public sector and by our union membership.

Rooted in both sections of the community in Northern Ireland, we are not immune to the denunciation of abortion which emanates from all churches and political parties in the north. Nevertheless the realisation that there had been no new evaluation of a law which ruled the lives of women more than 100 years ago and continues to do so, leaves us disturbed. When the life-threatening alternatives presented to our great-grandmothers are still amongst those sought out by women today, then condemnation is neither appropriate nor relevant.

Some of the most alarming evidence to surface in the project was not an indication of lack of progress, but an aggressive pattern of erosion of the progress of social provision achieved since the 1940s. The deliberate repression of improvements made in health care, education and social welfare was particularly disturbing for the women in the project. Not only had we all benefited from the reforms of post-war policy, but we are also employed in delivering the very services which are now in danger of extinction.

At first it sounded impossible that there should be any tendency to undermine the care and increased opportunity, which has been so carefully constructed over more than forty years, and was designed to ensure everyone a dignity and value, irrespective of class. However, evidence from our own experiences showed just how uncomfortably close the past had returned to cast its shadow on us.

Our hospital is dirty

Some of the most animated discussions which the project triggered during group workshops were in relation to the impact of the Tory government policy on the health, education and general economic status of working people in the last decade. The dramatic deterioration in the National Health Service led to inevitable comparisons with the elementary and financially prohibitive service available before the introduction of the post-war welfare state.

Rosaleen, a hospital domestic worker, compared her job and status to those of her predecessors, known as ward-maids.

Being involved in the Health and History project made me

111

more conscious of what was going on in my own hospital,
and increased my respect for my fellow workers. Ward-
maids weren't expected to have values or opinions. They
were just supposed to be work horses. They weren't seen
or appreciated. Today, with privatisation and competitive
tendering, we are being treated in the same way. Under
the guise of so-called efficiency, we are told that we have
to do more work for less money. And after seven years the
female domestics are still fighting to be recognised as
having equal value.

A biting observation which conveys the total lack of
responsibility of government cutbacks in hospitals was best
summed up when Rosaleen stated:

Many years ago, people didn't understand how essential
hygiene was for good health care. Today everyone knows
its importance, but the authorities aren't prepared to pay
for it. Our hospital is dirty.

The notorious community care scheme established by the
Thatcher government was concluded, by the group, to be nothing
other than a return to the days when families were left to cope
unsupported with the pressures and burdens of aging, invalid
relatives in need of specialised provision, but with only the
already overstretched resources of the family to rely on. The
emotional and economic weight of being a carer today, like then,
is almost exclusively carried by women.

The provision of essential equipment for hospital units is
increasingly being met by voluntary donations, from the
community which the hospital serves and by the endeavours of
patients' families and friends. The charitable element of hospital
care is a resurgent force in today's National Health Service, a
force which Aneurin Bevan's carefully constructed policies were
designed to make obsolete.

Mary, a long serving hospital worker, described community
care as,

112

Pushing patients out on a community with no resources. We are now experiencing some of the depression and fears our grandmothers must have felt for their families' futures, not knowing what was around the corner. Did we ever think we would see the day when we would have to have a whip around so that our children in need could have specialised care?

As the project's findings highlighted the return to familiar dilemmas and circumstances which we had associated with a less enlightened era, the tone of women's discussions swung from initial disbelief to one of anger.

Anna, a school meals worker said,

Competitive tendering has been horrendous for women. We are being pushed further and further back into the worst kind of part-time low paid jobs with bad conditions. The school meals service knows only too well what the consequences are for our women workers. And look at what's being done to the entire education system. The absolute essentials are crumbling: no money for books, not enough teachers, buildings in disrepair. It was education that got the working class off their knees and on their feet. That's why it is being destroyed.

These are not the words of a member of any radical left wing group, but the observations of a fifty-six year old woman who has spent twenty-two years working in school meals and representing her co-workers in the union branch through the dark demoralising days of private contractors and competitive tendering.

We often found ourselves pondering the lack of security for our futures. One woman observed how the possibility of 'saving up a wee nest egg for the future' has become almost impossible, because everything we earned was needed for the essentials. Women from working class communities today, like their grandmothers before them in the mills, fields and kitchens of the upper classes are not working for the 'little extras' or 'pin money',

113

but are often the sole breadwinners in families.

We won't be pushed out of history

It became clear to us, as we delved into the realities of women's lives that they were the pivotal centre around which working class life in Northern Ireland revolved: holding families together, providing for their material needs, contributing to the household income (sometimes the only income came from women), responsible for finding accommodation and ministering to the health of all the family members. In many of our own experiences, this was still the case. Yet we found ourselves wondering why, given the central role of women to the survival of working class communities, so much of the information has been obscured? Why did we have to go digging up such essential facts about women's lives?

Other women in other places have asked similar questions. Today it is widely acknowledged that the prevailing male definition of what is historically significant has caused the vital contribution of half the human race to be largely erased from history. The emergence of feminist historians has begun to redress the balance. We are not trained historians and some of us may still be shy about describing ourselves as feminists, but we know why we began the exploration into the history of the women in our families and communities. At a weekend school in Derry, one woman accurately conveyed the necessity for the Health and History project, when she said:

Women can't move forward until we understand where we've been in the past.

The Health and History project personalised for each of us the consequences of what Margaret Ward so pointedly refers to as 'the collective amnesia of male historians'. We began with an urgency borne of direct witness, a review of our own areas of activism, to find ways of ensuring that the future visibility of women does not fall victim to further relapses of amnesia. 'Women in the future shouldn't have to go looking for us: we won't be pushed out of history again', were common refrains at the closing workshops.

114

Reflections on the victories we had won within the trade union movement; the election of women to positions traditionally monopolised by men; the arduous, continuing battle to secure priorities of low-paid women workers on the negotiating agenda, led us to analyse the requirements for sustaining these victories in the future. If each time we took some new space not usually given to women, the victory would be a hollow one if the boundaries of that space were restricted to one woman's occupancy. The space taken must be expanded to embrace and accommodate the women still to come.

Our understanding of our role today within the trade union movement has been influenced by the process undertaken with the Health and History project. The project became the key to the vault of women's past experiences which until then had been closed to us. The history we uncovered revealed our inheritance in a female rite of passage. Each new generation of women add to that collective knowledge but access to its existence and the strength of its lessons will remain available only if we use the lessons now to direct our future actions.

Women have endured trials which must never be repeated, hardships which should no longer be a reality for any woman and a practice of marginalisation which almost lost them to us forever. Hardships and marginalisation are still unfortunately a reality in women's lives today. We are struggling to resist the policies of a government which appears hell-bent on returning us to a condition of existence which condemned many of our foremothers to a life of poverty and invisibility. We have learned from our history that the campaigns we are engaged in today as women trade unionists are the means of safeguarding the process of decades and the cement for the foundation of all our future visions.

The task we set ourselves when we first embarked upon the Health and History project was to make visible to ourselves women's lost history. We hope we have achieved that in even a small way. In the process we have discovered much about ourselves, and about the wider politics we create by how we live our own lives. Our task now is to keep visible our present struggles, so that we do not disappear into the shadows of the past and our history be unknown to our daughters.

Women Health & History - Resources

The questions and answers which formed the pool of information from which this book emerged are laid out in the following pages.

The Women Health and History project was the working title for the project used by NUPE Women's Committee as they travelled, holding workshops and gathering information.

The following pages are reproduced as they appeared during the project and the feedback from women in workshops is included here as a record of women's voices over the period 1900 - 1990.

Many of the memories evoked in each section of this short book clearly indicate the need for more extensive research and further exploration of women's own stories. Such research has already begun. ...

Women Health and History Workshop

Suggested Programme for 2 Day Workshop

Day 1   **Identifying the Sources**

Activity 1   Introduction - 'Breaking the Ice' 30 minute
                   group discusion and report back

Activity 2   'Finding the Sources'
                   $1^1/_2$ hour discussion and report back.

Activity 3   'Using history sources - Memories'
                   $1^1/_2$ hour discussion on interview techniques
                   and report back.

Activity 4   'Conducting interviews'
                   $1^1/_2$ hour session of paired interviews
                   followed by group discussion.

Day 2   **Collecting Oral Histories**

Activity 5   'Dig where you stand'
                   2-3 hour activity gathering oral histories of
                   group members
                   Two hour report back and discussion.

Sample Worksheet for Group Discussion Activity 1

Women Health & History

'Breaking the Ice'

Activity   Introduction

Aims   To introduce everyone on the course and to ensure full participation

Task   Interview the person beside you, asking the following questions:-

1. Name
2. Job/workplace
3. Length of time in the union
4. Union positions held
5. If the health service was to disappear tomorrow, in what way would your life be affected?

Sample Worksheet for Group Discussion Activity 2

Women Health & History

'Finding the Sources'

Activity   Finding the sources

Aims   To help us discover how our own history is
made and how we find out information
about it.

Task   In your group discuss the types of people, places
and objects which would help us make up a
picture of women and health.

Make a list on the flip chart provided and elect
someone to report back to the course.

Sample Flipchart A: from Group Discussion on Activity 2

'Finding the Sources'

What the workshop said

TYPE OF PEOPLE	PLACES TO LOOK TO FOR INFORMATION	USEFUL OBJECTS
Relatives		Papers
Friends	Libraries	Records
Teachers	Somerset House	Photographs
Organising bodies	Cultra folk Museum	Utensils
Historians	Peoples' houses (attics)	Books
Health visitors	Cemeteries	Television
Nursing officers	Hospitals	Old Insurance Policies
Family doctors	Transport Museum	Receipts
Retired midwives	Convents	Headstones
Retired district nurse	Universities	Clothes
Grave diggers	Schools	Furniture
Undertakers	City Hall	Crockery
Nuns	Church	
Farmers (haymaking, potato picking, no schooling		
Home help		
Postmen		

Sample Flipcharts A and B are from handwritten lists of potential sources identified by two different groups of women working in a workshop discussion

Sample Flipchart B: from Group Discussion on Activity 2

'Finding the Sources'

What the workshop said

PEOPLE	PLACES	OBJECTS
Anyone who lived before health service came in.	In their homes	Photographs
People who campaigned for implementation of health service.	In their clubs	Books
Relatives who are left after whole families were wiped out, through TB etc.	In your own branch	Household utensils
We think personal contact is the most important.	Senior citizens club	Tin baths
Retired teachers.	Community centres	Wash boards
Clergymen, School Inspectors.	Home helps can learn from their old people	Jug basin dressers
Any other charitable organisations in all areas.	Most important is to take time to listen	Cradles
Any retired pawnbrokers.		Melted soap
Corner shops - people paid for their groceries weekly.		Outdoor?
Local handywoman eg washing the dead, delivering babies.		No electric
Money lenders		No hot water
Coalman		Cooking on hobs, brick; stone jars
		Electric washing machine
		Hot water
		Electric iron
		Bathrooms
		Extra bedrooms
		Electric blankets

Sample Worksheet for Group Discussion Activity 3

Women Health & History

'Using the Sources - Memories'

Activity	Using History Sources - 'Memories'
Aims	To help us work out interviewing techniques for a history project and to identify 'key' questions for a successful interview.
Task	You are preparing a questionnaire to help you interview a friend about her personal health experiences over the years. In your group discuss what questions you would ask to produce a successful interview? Make a list of questions on the flip chart provided and elect someone to report back to the group.

Sample Flipcharts C, D and E record the skills women identified as important for individual or group interviews and listed a number of areas they wanted information on. Flipcharts E and F set out specific questions for individual interviews of women in the family.

Sample Flipchart C: from Group Discussion Activity 3

'Interviewing Skills Needed'

What the workshop said

Good listener

Memory/imagination

Note taking

Report back/public speaking

Confidence

Break the ice

Involve everyone

Collective exercise

Sample Flipchart D: from Group Discussion Activity 3

'What We Want to Know'

What the workshop said

Ask about illness, treatment,
and medication, cost.
Attitude of doctors,
Self help
Spirits for sprains,
Castor oil for everything
Senna pods
Syrup of figs
Poultice (bread, coal, sugar,
linseed)
Mustard baths for babies
Lack of sexual knowledge
Diphtheria
Scarlet Fever
Meningitis
Hospital fear (workhouse)
Mental illness
Handicapped children (curse)
Deformities

Personal health
Family health
Difference to her health by
health service
Longer life span
Plastic Surgery
Make Health Service better
Better health service
Progress for women in cancer
and serious illnesses.

Sample Flipchart E: from Group Discussion Activity 3

'What We Want to Know'

What the workshop said

Memories

First memories of having treatment or any member of family

Dental treatment
Inoculations
Visits by school nurses
Visits by doctors
Hospital treatment

First visit for any health treatment on your own. Any teenage experience. Example:

First period
Any sexual or hygiene education at school?
Having children, what type of care: happy or unhappy about it?
Ask her opinion on the changes in the medical treatment between then and now.

Sample Worksheet for Group Discussion Activity 4

Women Health & History

'Conducting Interviews'

Activity	Interviewing
Aim	To give us practice in conducting an interview and to help us find out if we can succeed in getting the type of information we really want.
	To give us the experience of using notes and tape recorders.
Task	In pairs, pick one person to be the interviewer and the other to be interviewed. You want to find out what sort of health care was available for women when they were at school.
	Take a few minutes to talk over the questions, then, using the tape recorder and your notes conduct a five minute interview.

Sample of one woman's interview notes in preparation for a tape recorded interview

Preparation

Target dates, events

Key questions ready before interview:

Name/age/school

Do you remember the doctor coming to school?

Do you remember ever being sick?

What age did you take your first period?

Were you prepared?

How did it feel?

What age did you leave school?

Were there lunches?

Age married? When first baby?

Any ante-natal care?

Any frightening stories 'Old Wives Tales'?

Memories of you/family sickness? What types?

Women Health & History - Questionnaire

Sample questionnaire prepared from the collective group report backs

Married Women

1 Name and age?

2 Do you remember your first day at school?

3 Do you remember the doctor/nurse coming to the school? How did you feel about them?

4 When you were a child, did you ever have to go to hospital? Were you frightened?

5 What age were you when you had your first period? Were you prepared and how did you feel? Were you frightened by any old wives tales?

6 What age were you when you first went out with boys?

7 How did your parents feel about it?

8 Did you receive any sex education at school?

9 What age were you when you left school?

10 What age were you when you first started work?

11 How did you feel about working with men?

12 What age were you when you got married?

13 How did you feel on your honeymoon night? What was your first home luxury, ie washing machine etc.?

14 When did you have your first baby? Did you receive any maternity benefits?

15 Did you have any health problems during your pregnancy?

16 How did you find your ante-natal care?

17 Were you frightened of labour and what was your reaction to it?

18 Was your husband present at labour and how did he feel?

19 Do you think there is adequate provision for post natal care?

20 Did you suffer from post natal depression? Did you receive any medical help?

21 How did your husband and family react to you?

22 Do you think that the mothers of today should have a choice, if medically safe, of having their baby at home?

23 Did you experience any health problems in your own family? How did you and your family deal with them?

24 Do you think that women abuse medication and drugs?

25 Do you think that we should rely more on old remedies or cures?

26 What are your views on modern methods of family planning?

27 How do you feel about the influence of television on today's youth and family life in general, ie videos?

28 What do you think of the health service now?

29 How do you think privatisation will affect you when it is introduced into the health service?

Sample Flipchart F: from Group Discussion Activity 4

Notes for Interviewing

What the workshop said

Outline names and aims

Find out about deceased family members

Age at death?

Did they get medical attention?

Most important - make people feel at ease

Ask about childbirth

Did she have baby at home?

Did she have handywomen or midwife?

Did she attend doctor during pregnancy and have to pay for treatment?

Did she have any after care?

What medicine did children have?

What was dental care like?

Was deafness acknowledged?

Did they receive any maternity grants or allowances?

Any death grants?

What social life they had?

What was her first luxury? Was it electric light, radio, inside toilet or running water?

Sample Worksheet for Group Discussion Activity 5

Women Health and History

'Dig where you stand'

Activity   Collecting oral histories

Aims   To collect the oral histories of the women in the
group based on their own experience and their
memories of the lives of their mothers and
grandmothers.

Task   1. In your group take a blank flipchart (see
sample blank flipchart of 'Dig where you stand'
on next page) and list the decades on the left,
starting with 1900.

2. Across the top enter the follwing headings:
Family Health
Housing and Diet
Health care - official and unofficial
Childbirth and Contraception
Sex

3. Pick someone to write key words in
appropriate boxes and to report back.

4. Begin recounting your memories under each
heading, starting with the earliest decade.

Sample Blank Flipchart of 'Dig Where you Stand'

	FAMILY HEALTH	HOUSING & DIET	HEALTH CARE OFFICIAL/ UNOFFICIAL	CHILDBIRTH & CONTRACEP -TION	SEX
1900 -1910					
1910 -1920					
1920 -1930					
1930 -1940					
1940 -1950					
1950 -1960					
1960 -1970					
1970 -1980					
1980 -1990					

The following pages contain sample flipcharts with the
comments and information colllected from women
at a 'Dig where you stand' workshop

DATE	FAMILY HEALTH	CHANGES
1900 - 10	LARGE FAMILY: FLITTING AND HAND CARTS: WOMEN IN HOME: CONSUMPTION/LOWER LIFE EXPECTANCY GRANDMOTHER DIED IN CHILDBIRTH/HOME BIRTHS	
1910 - 20	FLU - GRANDMOTHER SURVIVED DEATHS TB - HANDICAPPED - NO TREATMENT - FAMILY 'SLUR'. CONTAGIOUS DISEASES - ISOLATION/ OUTHOUSES. RICKETS COMMON. MENTAL ILLNESS - TREATMENT? DEATHS IN HOME - PAWNING - SMOGS - CHEST PROBLEMS	
1920 - 30		
1930 - 40	MOTHER SCARLET FEVER - ISOLATION WARDS - FEVER HOSPITAL - POLIO - WHOOPING COUGH - OUTDOOR RELIEF - GP - HOUSECALLS - PAYMENTS - CONCEALMENT RE MENSTRUATION - RATIONING	WAR
1940 - 50	NHS - FREE CARE: PRESCRIPTIONS; DENTAL CARE; GLASSES; GP VISITS; HOSPITALS - IMMUNISATION SCHOOL NURSES - PRIMARY SCHOOLS	MORE HOSPITAL DEATHS/BIRTHS - HOUSING
1950 - 60	SCHOOL DINNERS - ORANGE JUICE - SPECIAL SCHOOLS - COD LIVER OIL - HOUSING ESTATES SPIRALLING VIROL- UP - EARLY 50'S - HEALTH VISITING	
1960 - 70	IMMUNISATION - WHOOPING COUGH - PRESCRIPTION CHARGES - SEX EDUCA- TION (NOT OFFICIAL) - HOME HELPS - SOCIAL WELFARE BENEFITS - HEALTH BABIES (POST WAR EFFECT) - CHILD- BIRTH - INDUCTIONS	
1970 - 80	TORIES 'MILK SNATCHERS' - CLEAN AIR ZONES - CUTS HOSPITAL SERVICES START	
1980	CUTS - CONTINUE - MAJOR CUTS - SELF AWARENESS - HEALTH - ALTERNATIVE MEDICINE - NATURAL CHILDBIRTH - PRESSURE DEMANDS FROM WOMEN	

DATE	OFFICIAL &UNOFFICIAL CARE	CHANGES
1900 - 10	MEDICAL CARE WAS UNAVAILABLE TO WORKING CLASS, ALWAYS A HANDYWOMAN IN AREA - THE POOR PEOPLE HELPED EACH OTHER BY COLLECTING MONEY TO PAY FOR MEDICAL CARE FOR SERIOUSLY ILL CHILDREN.	
1910 - 20	PEOPLE STILL DEPENDED ON OLD REMEDIES AND CHARITY - CHILD BIRTH WAS STILL A HIT AND MISS AFFAIR - HIGH MORTALITY RATE - WORKING CLASS RIDDLED WITH TB DIARRHEA AND UNNAMED DISEASES.	
1920 - 30	PEOPLE STARTED TO USE THEIR OWN FORMS OF FUMIGATION (BURNING BEDDING AND SULPHUR CANDLES) STILL DEPENDING ON HANDYWOMEN FOR CHILDBIRTH AND WASHING DEAD - OLD FASHIONED REMEDIES STILL USED FOR SERIOUS ILLNESS.	
1930 - 40	SEES BEGINNING OF HEALTH SERVICE - CHILDREN ISSUED WITH MALT, COD LIVER OIL, DENTAL CARE - PEOPLE STILL VISITED THE DISPENSARIES AND STILL HAD TO PAY FOR MEDICINES - COUGH BOTTLE GIVEN FOR EVERYTHING.	
1940 - 50	THE BEGINNING OF THE CONTAGIOUS DISEASES BEING ERADICATED - DISTRICT NURSE VISITING HOMES OF SICK AND BEDRIDDEN - HEALTH SERVICE ESTABLISHED - FREE VISITS TO GPS, DENTISTS - OAPS GIVEN CONCESSIONS.	FREE DINNERS GIVEN TO POOR CHILDREN - CHILDREN'S HEALTH SHOWS IMPROVEMENT.
1950 - 60	HANDICAPPED AND MENTALLY ILL BROUGHT OUT OF THE DARK - DAY CARE CENTRES ESTABLISHED ON A LOCAL BASIS - SPECIALISED DOCTORS BROUGHT TO THE FORE.	WOMEN'S DISORDERS BROUGHT INTO OPEN
1960 - 70	MORE HELP FOR OAP'S AND CHILDREN - MEALS ON WHEELS - REALISED THAT FOOD ADDITIVES WERE CAUSING ALLERGIES AND FORMS OF CANCER.	MORE HOMES / CENTRES FOR HANDICAPPED AND ELDERLY ESTABLISHED.
1970 - 80	PEOPLE STARTED TO REALISE THE SHORTCOMINGS OF HEALTH SERVICE - MORE MONEY NEEDED TO BE SPENT BUT GOVERNMENTS REFUSED TO BUDGE.	CANCER ESPECIALLY AMONG WOMEN RECOGNISED AS MAJOR THREAT.

DATE	HOUSING AND DIET	CHANGES
1900 - 10	TIED HOUSING (RURAL AREAS) - POOR DIET LEADING TO TB AND RICKETS - NO RUNNING WATER/OUTSIDE TOILETS - EMIGRATION TO USA/SCOTLAND/ ENGLAND.	
1910 - 20	CHILDREN DYING FROM MALNUTRITION - WAR SHILLING A DAY FOR WIVES OF SOLDIERS - LOW PAY - NO HOUSE BUILDING.	
1920 - 30	MASS UNEMPLOYMENT AND STARVATION (DEPRESSION) - MEN JOINED (FREE STATE ARMY) TO FEED FAMILIES - FAMILIES SEPARATED FOR LONG PERIOD OF TIME - STILL NO IMPROVEMENT IN HOUSE BUILDING.	
1930 - 40	PREFABS - WAR - FOOD RATIONING/ CLOTHING RATIONED - POOR SOLD COUPONS FOR MONEY - RURAL AREAS PEOPLE SWAPPED EGGS/BUTTER FOR OTHER NEEDS.	BLACK MARKET STARTED - MONEY MADE BY SMUGGLERS
1940 - 50	STILL WAR - TOWN AREAS HAD INTRODUCED SCHOOL MEALS - HEALTH SERVICE CAME INTO BEING - WARTIME FOOD POOR BUT ADEQUATE FOR NOURISHMENT - EMIGRATION TO AUSTRALIA.	
1950 - 60	1951 SCHOOL MEALS COST 12½P PER WEEK - HOUSING IMPROVED INDOOR TOILETS/RUNNING WATER - STANDARD OF LIVING IMPROVED, TV/WASHING MACHINES STATUS SYMBOL CAR - HOUSING TRUST/COUNCIL - RURAL RENT £2.16 PER WEEK	
1960 - 70	REDEVELOPMENT OF SLUMS STARTED - DIED IMPROVED - FOREIGN FOODS BEING EATEN BY HOLIDAY MAKER - INCREASING DEMAND GRANTS FOR HOME IMPROVEMENTS STILL PREFABS.	TERRACE HOUSES BOUGHT FOR £475
1970 - 80	BETTER HOUSING - PEOPLE MOVING TO RURAL AREAS AS NEED FOR HOUSES IS ON THE INCREASE - JUNK FOOD ON THE INCREASE - RENT/RATES STRIKE BROUGHT INTO BEING P.O.D.A. (ENFORCED) - FAST FOODS - OBESITY ON INCREASE.	F.I.S. INTRODUCED

DATE	HOUSING AND DIET(cont.)	CHANGES
1980	CUT BACKS IN HOUSING EX BUILDINGS - RENTS NOW HIGHER (£18 - 50 WEEKLY RURAL) - SCHOOL MEALS NOW 70P PER DAY SERVICE IN DANGER - NOW 90% GETTING FREE SCHOOLS MEALS - STILL PREFABS - ADDITIVES TO FOOD ENDANGERING HEALTH - MORE PEOPLE ON FAMILY INCOME SUPPLEMENTS	

DATE	CHILDBIRTH and CONTRACEPTION	CHANGES
1900 - 10	LARGE FAMILIES - MOTHERS/CHILDREN DYING - HANDYWOMEN - INSANITY/ POST-NATAL DEPRESSION - NO KNOWLEDGE OF CONTRACEPTION - ALWAYS UNMARRIED MOTHER - BREAST FEEDING.	
1910 - 20	AUNT DISAPPEARED WHEN SHE BECAME PREGNANT - SENT AWAY OR PUT INTO MENTAL HOME (WICKEDNESS) - INCEST - CHILD EVERY YEAR (NO MEDICAL AID) - KIDS IN BED/ CONTRACEPTION - FLOUR BAGS FOR NAPPIES.	WORLD WAR VD?
1920 - 30	HANDYWOMAN - MOTHERS STRAIGHT BACK TO WORK THIRD DAY OR SAME DAY - MADE THE CHILDCARE STUFF (PLAYPEN) TEA - CHEST DRAWERS - SHAWLS NOT PRAMS - ABORTION - GIN BATHS - SAVE STAMPS FOR DOCTOR/ AMBULANCE.	
1930 - 40	HANDYWOMAN - BOILING WATER - STILL NO TRIMMING/NHS - NO POST/ ANTENATAL CARE - NO ELECTRIC - LOT OF BLEEDING/NO MEN INVOLVED - CASTOR OIL - DIDN'T TELL MOTHER ABOUT PREGNANCY/EMBARRASSED - MAKING OUR OWN SANITARY TOWELS.	ELECTRICITY RUNNING WATER WORLD WAR II
1940 - 50	HANDYWOMEN - NURSE GALLAGHER - QUEEN STREET HOUSE FOR MIDWIVES OPERATION - OMAGH NURSE ON BICYCLE - HOME BIRTHS EMBARRASSMENT - DOCTOR NOT ALLOWED TO TOUCH BINDING.	NHS SOCIAL SECURITY PRESCRIPTIONS
1950 - 60	HOSPITAL BIRTHS - SMALLER FAMILIES? - WE WERE BORN AT HOME MOTHERS AFRAID OF HOSPITALS EMBARRASSMENT DIDN'T WANT TO SEE DOCTOR - REMEDIES FOR MORNING SICKNESS - FAMILY ALLOWANCE - INCREASE IN BIRTH? BINDERS: MATERNITY GRANT - NEVER CHANGES - SANITARY TOWELS/CHEMISTS.	

DATE	CHILDBIRTH and CONTRACEPTION (cont.)	CHANGES
1960 - 70	HOSPITAL BIRTHS - FREE ORANGE JUICE/MILK/MALT - BABY CLINICS/ INJECTIONS - MALONE PLACE - BAD IMAGE OF MATERNITY HOSPITAL - THALIDOMIDE - ACCESS TO CONTRACEPTION - ALWAYS WOMEN TAKING PRECAUTIONS - SOME SEX EDUCATION.	SEX EDUCATION
1970 - 80	SOME DOCTORS WANT HOME BIRTHS AGAIN - FIRST FAMILY PLANNING CLINIC OMAGH/BELFAST - KNOWLEDGE - EMBARRASSED GOING - HOSPITAL - CATTLE MARKET - HYSTERECTOMIES - INDUCTION - BIRTH DEFECTS - STERILISATION/VASECTOMIES (GETTING CAUGHT ON).	MATERNITY LAWS/WOMEN'S RIGHTS
1980	THINGS IN HOSPITALS IMPROVE - NOW IN AND OUT IN HOURS - NOW YOU HAVE TO HAVE A RANGE OF EXPENSIVE THINGS.	

DATE	SEX	CHANGES
1900 - 10	OLD WIVES HORROR TALES/WOMEN WITH HEARTBURN IS SAID TO HAVE A CHILD BORN WITH A LOT OF HAIR/ WOMEN NOT ALLOWED TO CROSS THEIR LEGS	NOT A LOT OF CHANGE
1910 - 20	LACK OF KNOWLEDGE DUE TO EDUCATION SEX/HEALTH BECAUSE OF LACK OF KNOWLEDGE FROM MALES, WOMEN'S HEALTH SUFFERED	SEX EDUCATION CLASSES
1920 - 30	PEOPLE WERE STILL VERY IGNORANT OF THE FACTS SURROUNDING SEX AND FOUND IT DIFFICULT TO PUT INTO WORDS	TV & VIDEO ARE A KNOWLEDGE UNTO THEMSELVES
1930 - 40	PEOPLE HID THE FACT THAT THEY WERE PREGNANT AND STRAPPED THEMSELVES UP. THIS IS SAID TO HAVE CAUSED DEFORMITY IN BABIES	WOMEN NOW WORE LOOSE CLOTHING AND ARE PROUD OF THE FACT THAT THEY ARE PREGNANT
1940 - 50	PEOPLE NOW AWARE OF THE FACTS BUT STILL UNABLE TO SPEAK THESE FEARS/A LOT OF TALK ABOUT CONTRACEPTION AND BIRTH CONTROL BUT DO NOT KNOW IF ANY DAMAGE IS DONE	NOT A LOT OF CHANGE. DO WE STILL PUT THE BLAME ON EARLY DAYS?
1950 - 60	PEOPLE STILL THOUGHT THAT IF YOU WERE KISSED INTIMATELY OR TOUCHED IN THE KNEE THAT YOU WERE PREGNANT	
1960 - 70	WASHING OF HAIR OR PHYSICAL EXERCISE WAS TO BE AVOIDED. PEOPLE IGNORANT OF ORAL SEX SMOKING CAN CAUSE SMALL BABIES	THE OPPOSITE STEPS ARE TO BE TAKEN BECAUSE OF HEALTH AND CLEANLINESS
1970 - 80	MAYBE MORE ENLIGHTENED BUT STILL UNABLE TO TALK TO CHILDREN/BOOKS ARE NOW AVAILABLE FOR PARENTS TO GIVE TO CHILDREN TO READ. SEX EDUCATION FREELY AVAILABLE AT SCHOOL	CHILDREN NOW FIND OUT BEFORE PARENTS TELL THEM BECAUSE OF SEX EDUCATION IN SCHOOLS, TV AND VIDEOS
1980	CHILDREN COULD EDUCATE PARENTS ON SEX	